CONTEMPORARY COUNTERPOINT

THEORY & APPLICATION

To access audio visit:
www.halleonard.com/mylibrary

Enter Code
7537-9921-0817-5448

BETH DENISCH

ABOUT THE AUDIO

To access the accompanying audio, go to www.halleonard.com/mylibrary and enter the code found on the first page of this book. This will grant you instant access to every example. Examples with accompanying audio are marked with an audio icon.

BERKLEE PRESS

Editor in Chief: Jonathan Feist
Senior Vice President of Online Learning and Continuing Education/CEO of Berklee Online: Debbie Cavalier
Vice President of Enrollment Marketing and Management: Mike King
Vice President of Online Education: Carin Nuernberg
Editorial Assistants: Emily Jones, Eloise Kelsey
Cover Design: Ranya Karafilly
Back Cover Photo of Author: Susan Wilson

ISBN 978-0-87639-183-9

Press

1140 Boylston Street
Boston, MA 02215-3693 USA
(617) 747-2146

Visit Berklee Press Online at
www.berkleepress.com

Study music online at
online.berklee.edu

DISTRIBUTED BY

HAL•LEONARD®

7777 W. BLUEMOUND RD. P.O. BOX 13819
MILWAUKEE, WISCONSIN 53213

Visit Hal Leonard Online
www.halleonard.com

Berklee Press, a publishing activity of Berklee College of Music, is a not-for-profit educational publisher. Available proceeds from the sales of our products are contributed to the scholarship funds of the college.

CONTENTS

ACKNOWLEDGMENTS

Many people touched this book, directly and indirectly. Debbie Cavalier, senior vice president of online learning and continuing education, without whose support and encouragement the online course and this text would never have happened. Carin Nuernberg, vice president of online education, and Boriana Alexiev, senior director of online education, who worked with me step-by-step in authoring the online course and whose ongoing help and guidance are indispensible.

Special thanks to Jonathan Feist, at Berklee Press, for his consistent support throughout multiple deadlines and to Jonathan and his editorial team whose insights into focusing the topics and refining the writing style have significantly contributed to the quality of this book.

A number of colleagues have graciously shared their experiences and thoughts regarding content, including Arnold Friedman, former chair of the Berklee Composition Department, who took the time from his busy schedule and provided "spot on" reflections and suggestions. Prof. Marti Epstein, whose insightful feedback to my often rambling "Ahas!" while writing this text was really helpful. Prof. Richard Applin, who is deeply missed, encouraged me to develop this new, innovative approach to teaching counterpoint, to take the next step from his preceding *Tonal Counterpoint* text, and I am indebted to his counsel.

Thank you to all of my students, both on campus and around the world through Berklee Online, for discovering, mastering, and freely applying these contrapuntal techniques in new and exciting ways in your own creations. Your feedback has directly impacted the content of this book in both its ordering and prioritizing. From hundreds of students taught and thousands of assignments completed we are only able to share a few examples. Peer learning is a powerful pedagogical resource, and I am grateful for my students' willingness to share. Special thanks go to the following students who graciously allowed me to include their work: Andrey Borisov, Patrick Cupo, Ivan Jadresic, Emily Jones, Andrew Joslyn, Murat Kalaora, Juan Carlos Magsalin, Tim Hijenhuis, Julien Nodier, Eric Osanick, Jeff Penny, and Anita Wood.

My most profound thanks go to my partner, Betsy Breitborde, who recorded the audio examples for this book. Her music production expertise was indispensable and her lovingkindness and understanding supported me through all the ups and downs of book writing. And to my two cats, Tiger Balm Jack and Koshka Blueberry Jerry, for their companionship as well as for entertaining the online counterpoint students with spontaneous runway appearances across my desktop during our live streaming counterpoint video chats.

PART I: THE BASICS

The first section of this book, chapters 1 to 4, covers music theory and counterpoint basics. Chapter 1 presents musical textures and consonance/dissonance in relationship to intervals, melodies, chords, and non-chord tones. Chapter 2 examines musical form and an introduction to writing two-voice counterpoint. Chapter 3 explores the construction of melodies and how to manipulate the motive within the melodic line to more effectively express musical ideas. Chapter 4 explains how to create and use the simple canon, as a stand-alone technique and in a contrapuntal texture.

CHAPTER 1

Overview

WHAT IS COUNTERPOINT?

Counterpoint is two or more melodic lines working together to create music. In *contra-puntal music* (music created using counterpoint), each of the melodic lines—treble, bass, and every line in between—works independently as a melody as well as together harmonically.

These concurrent melodies create a texture called "polyphony." Polyphony and counterpoint have been around for about one thousand years and are at the root of melody and harmony in Western music. As such, understanding counterpoint is as important to contemporary music as it is to music history. In this book, we will study contemporary and traditional repertoire and applications that demonstrate counterpoint's power and effectiveness as a creative technique.

IDENTIFYING TEXTURES

"Texture" is used to describe the relative "thickness" or "thinness" of musical sound. Like the texture of fabric, musical textures can be rough or smooth, simple or complex, dense or sparse. Here are three basic musical textures, only one of which includes counterpoint.

Audio 1

Monophony is a solo melody, a single line of music and the simplest of musical textures (from the Greek: *mono*—one, and *phony*—sound or voice). Here are two examples. Each is to be played solo for a monophonic texture.

FIG. 1.1. Example of Monophonic Texture (Blues Melody)

The "Hu Jia Shi Ba Pai" melody dates back two thousand years and is attributed to Cai Wenji (Eastern Han Dynasty).

Hu Jia Shi Ba Pai

FIG. 1.2. Example of Monophonic Texture (Excerpt, Western notation)

Homophony is a melody with chords, as in a song—a harmonized melody. The chords (harmonies) do not stand on their own as independent melodies but are heard as shapes supporting or harmonizing the single melody (from the Greek: *homo*—same, and *phony*—sound or voice).

Audio 2

FIG. 1.3. Example of Homophonic Texture

Polyphony is *more* than one melody happening at the same time. The three-part contrapuntal textures in figures 1.4 and 1.5 each contain two treble melodies and one bass melody that all work together to create beautiful harmonies while at the same time maintaining their melodic independence from each other. That is, multiple layers are heard separately and simultaneously (from the Greek: *poly*—many, and *phony*—sound or voice).

"Look for the Silver Lining," by Buddy DeSylva and Jerome Kern, arranges nicely for three voices. Figure 1.4 demonstrates measures 1–8; the original melody is in the middle voice.

Audio 3

FIG. 1.4. Example of Polyphonic Texture, Jazz Style

And the famous Baroque composer Barbara Strozzi's "Mercé di voi" is another excellent example. Available recordings include "Canto di Bella Bocca," Barbara Strozzi, *Strozzi: Il Primo Libro de Madrigali, Op. 1*; Orlando di Lasso Ensemble, Bella Musica (2000).

Sonetto proemio dell'opera
Mercé di voi

Barbara Strozzi

FIG. 1.5. Example of Polyphonic Texture, Baroque Style

CONSONANCE AND DISSONANCE

Consonance and *dissonance* refer to greater and lesser degrees of relaxation and decreases and increases in tension, respectively. However, different styles of music through the ages have redefined these levels of stability. For example, in the contemporary metal styles, consonance and dissonance may refer more directly to the amount of distortion happening at any given time rather than the pitches being used. Or, in Medieval and Renaissance music, the interval of the third (e.g., C and E) was considered imperfect, and more dissonant than a perfect fifth (e.g., C and G). An interval is the distance between any two pitches. The intervals of the second and seventh are treated with a high degree of stability in several folk styles of the Eastern European traditions while they are historically considered dissonant in the Western European classical tradition. So, to some extent, one's culture and experiences temper the perception of that dissonant clash or consonant pleasantness.

Many consider the Baroque period (ca. 1600–1750) to be the apex for contrapuntal accomplishment. Creating counterpoint to sound like this style requires following very strict rules about what is considered consonant and dissonant and how to apply those principles correctly. If you are scoring for a movie cue set in eighteenth-century Europe, you may want to follow these rules. If you are looking for some new lines in a contemporary piece, then following those specific rules may not be your concern.

All styles of music can use counterpoint, and you are encouraged to explore how these contrapuntal techniques can be applied to your original music. In your own writing, and in listening to others' music, it is important to recognize varying levels of consonance and dissonance. The next three pieces demonstrate different levels of consonance and dissonance.

Play through them, if you can play scores, or seek out recordings, such as those mentioned.

1. The beginning of Vivaldi's "Spring" movement from *The Four Seasons* is very consonant. Available recordings include *Vivaldi: The Four Seasons*; Joshua Bell and Academy of St. Martin-in-the-Fields, Sony Classics (2008).

Spring
from *The Four Seasons, Concerto, Op. 8, No. 1*

Antonio Vivaldi

FIG. 1.6. "La Primavera" from *Concerto in E Major for Violin, String Orchestra and Continuo* by Antonio Vivaldi, Measures 1–4

2. The beginning of the "Adagio" from Mozart's *String Quartet in C Major, KV. 465* is dissonant but in a late eighteenth-century Classical style. Available recordings include *Mozart–100 Supreme Classical Masterpieces*; Salzburg Mozarteum Quartet, X5 Music Group (2011).

Quartet No. 19 in C Major
K. 465

FIG. 1.7. "Adagio" from *String Quartet No. 19 in C Major, K. 465* by W.A. Mozart, Measures 1–8

3. Here is the children's song "Ring a Ring o' Roses" (or "Ring Around the Rosie") harmonized in a more chromatic fashion, lifting it out of a consonant framework. The modified melody is in the middle voice.

Audio 4

Ring a Ring o' Roses

FIG. 1.8. "Ring a Ring o' Roses" Traditional. Chromatic arrangement.

IDENTIFYING INTERVALS

Intervals describe the distance between two notes. We mentioned them in passing during the consonance and dissonance section. Figure 1.9 shows the distances (in semitones), the names (in quality and quantity) of frequently used simple intervals, and their common abbreviations.

NUMBER OF SEMITONES	COMMON INTERVAL NAMES	ABBREVIATIONS
0	Unison	P1
1	Minor Second	m2
2	Major Second	M2
3	Minor Third	m3
4	Major Third	M3
5	Perfect Fourth	P4
6	Tritone: Augmented Fourth, Diminished Fifth	a4 or d5
7	Perfect Fifth	P5
8	Minor Sixth	m6
9	Major Sixth	M6
10	Minor Seventh	m7
11	Major Seventh	M7
12	Perfect Octave	P8

FIG. 1.9. Interval Identification Table

CONSONANT AND DISSONANT INTERVALS IN THE BAROQUE ERA

FIG. 1.10. Baroque Consonant/Dissonant Interval Table

Activity 1.1. Match the Textures and Dissonance Levels

Match the type of texture and level of consonance or dissonance with the following examples (audio track 5). Answers are at the end of this chapter.

TEXTURE	CONSONANT/DISSONANT
Polyphonic	Very Consonant
Monophonic	Slightly Dissonant (Basically Consonant)
Homophonic	Dissonant
	Not Applicable

FIG. 1.11. Activity 1.1

Audio 5

FIG. 1.12. Activity 1.1.

NON-CHORD TONES

How do we know when to use a consonant interval or a dissonant interval? One way is to place consonant notes that are chord members in more prominent rhythmic positions and to carefully prepare for and move away from notes that are non-chord tones. Non-chord tones are often, but not always, dissonances. Any note that does not belong to the chord is called a "non-chord tone." Chord tones support the harmony and non-chord tones help make the lines melodic.

Traditional non-chord tones can be divided into two groups: (1) those that are approached and resolved by *step* or the same note, and (2) those that are approached or resolved by *leap*. All non-chord tones are prepared with a consonant chord tone and resolved with a consonant chord tone. This grouping of notes (CT–NCT–CT) is called a "figure." All of these figures must begin with a consonant chord tone, the note of preparation, and end with a consonant chord tone, the note of resolution.

Group 1: NCTs approached and resolved by step or the same note

NON-CHORD TONE	ABBREVIATION	DEFINITION
Passing Tone	PT	Approach and resolve by step in the same direction.
Neighbor Tone	NT	Approach and resolve by step in the opposite direction.
Double Passing Tone	DPT	Approach and resolve with three steps in the same direction, middle two notes are the DPTs.
Double Neighbor Tone	DNT	Approach by step, then leap by a third in the opposite direction and resolve by step to the original note, middle two notes are the DNTs.
Suspension	Sus	Approach by the same note (chord changes) and resolve down by step on a weaker beat or weaker portion of a beat.
Retardation	R	Approach by the same note (chord changes) and resolve up by step.
Anticipation	Ant	Approach by step and resolve by the same note (chord changes).
Pedal Tone	PedTn	Approach and resolve by the same note (chords change).

FIG. 1.13. Non-Chord Tones Group 1

Passing tones and neighbor tones may be the most commonly used non-chord tones. The Italian folk song "Giovanottina Che Vieni alla Fonte" uses both types. Review this melody and notice the differences between passing and neighbor tones.

Audio 6

FIG. 1.14. Melody with Passing and Neighbor Tones

Group 2: NCTs approached or resolved by leap

NON-CHORD TONE	ABBREVIATION	DEFINITION
Appogiatura	App	Approach by leap and resolve by step in the opposite direction often on a weaker beat or weaker portion of a beat.
Escape Tone	ET	Approach by step and resolve by leap in the opposite direction.
Cambiata	C	Approach by step then leap a third in the same direction and then resolve by step in the opposite direction, middle two notes are C.

FIG. 1.15. Non-Chord Tones Group 2

"Yellow Quinces" is a *sevdah*, a type of Bosnian folk song. It contains non-chord tones from both categories.

Yellow Quinces
Zute dunje

Audio 7

FIG. 1.16. Melody with Non-Chord Tones

Activity 1.2

Identify the circled non-chord tones in the following melody. Answers are at the end of this chapter.

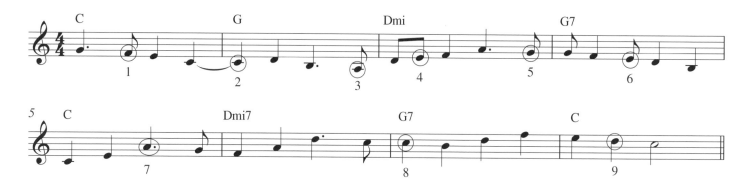

FIG. 1.17. Activity 1.2

CONTEMPORARY MUSIC EXAMPLES

So far, we have looked at texture, consonance/dissonance, and non-chord tones. Listen to one or more of your favorite songs and ask yourself:

- Are there monophonic, homophonic, or polyphonic textures in this music?

- Is this music mostly consonant or somewhat or extremely dissonant?

- If there are melodies in the music, listen to how they support the harmonic progression by featuring chord tones. What kind of non-chord tones do you hear in these melodies?

- Here are a few examples of some contemporary pieces that include polyphonic sections:

  1. "God Only Knows," Brian Wilson and Tony Asher, *Pet Sounds*; Beach Boys, Capital Records (1966).

  2. "Tell Me Something Good," Wonder, *Rags to Rufus*; Rufus and Chaka Khan, ABC Records (1974).

  3. "Welcome to Europe," Tom Jenkinson, *Hello Everything*; Squarepusher, Warp Records (2006).

  4. "Elected," Alice Cooper, *Mascara & Monsters: The Best of Alice Cooper*; Rhino Records (2001).

  5. "Word Up!" Lawrence Ernest Blackmon & Thomas Michael Jenkins, *Word Up!*; Cameo, Atlanta Artists (1986).

6. "Fugue," Friedrich Gulda, *Then and Now*; Emerson, Lake & Palmer, Eagle, 1998 (Sanctuary Midline, 2006).

7. "Fracture," Robert Fripp, *Starless and Bible Black*; King Crimson, Island (E.G.) Records (1974).

8. "Lightning Rod," Jerry Reed, *East Bound and Down*; Jerry Reed, RCA (1977).

9. "Two Weeks," Droste, Rossen, Taylor and Bear, *Veckatimest*; Grizzly Bear, Warp Records (2009).

10. "The Prophet's Song," Brian May, *A Night at the Opera*; Queen, EMI Parlophone (Europe), Elektra (U.S.), 1975.

SUMMARY

In this chapter, you learned to identify a music's texture and that counterpoint, or writing contrapuntally, uses the polyphonic texture. The consonant/dissonant spectrum was examined and you understood these differences by listening to and reading music from different style periods. Intervals were introduced and non-chord tones were defined and identified in various melodies.

ACTIVITY ANSWERS

Activity 1.1. Answers

1. Polyphonic, Dissonant, 2. Homophonic, Slightly Dissonant, 3. Polyphonic, Very Consonant, 4. Monophonic, Not Applicable

Activity 1.2. Answers

1. Passing tone (PT), 2. Retardation (R), 3. Escape tone (ET), 4. Passing tone (PT), 5. Anticipation (Ant), 6. Passing tone (PT), 7. Appogiatura (App), 8. Suspension (Sus), 9. Passing tone (PT).

CHAPTER 2

Writing Counterpoint

Effective counterpoint features strong melodic lines with independent rhythms. In addition, the pitches and rhythms must also work well in harmonic and rhythmic combination. An important part of securing this success is to be aware of the harmonic implications and proportional rhythmic durations between voices. Paying attention to these factors allows a higher level of control from which you can more effectively communicate your musical ideas.

RHYTHMIC RATIOS AND SPECIES COUNTERPOINT[1]

Species counterpoint is the traditional method of teaching counterpoint that identifies the voices' rhythmic relationships to each other. It also defines how to use consonance and dissonance to get that traditional sound. The following table summarizes basic rhythmic aspects of species counterpoint. (Note: species counterpoint does not directly address rests.) The musical examples in this table also adhere to the traditional rules of consonance and dissonance that correctly position the chord tones and non-chord tones for traditional harmonic usage.

Species 1 (Ratio 1:1)

Audio 8

The bass and treble voices use the same note durations. This is the rhythmic ratio of 1:1.

FIG. 2.1. Species 1

---

1 The musical examples in figures 2.1 through 2.5 are typical but not specific to any particular text other than figures 2.1 and 2.2(a) from *A Treatise on Simple Counterpoint in Forty Lessons*, by Friederich J. Lehmann (1907), figures 6 and 17, respectively.

Species 2 (Ratio 2:1, 3:1)

One voice has two or three notes for each single note in the other voice. The 3:1 ratio also works well in triple meter. Examples (b) and (c) include unequal rhythmic divisions and syncopations.

(a) Ratio 2:1

(b) Ratio 3:1

(c) Ratio 3:1 (Triple Meter)

FIG. 2.2. Species 2

Species 3 (Ratio 4:1)

One voice has four notes for each single note in the other voice. This is the rhythmic ratio of 4:1.

FIG. 2.3. Species 3

Species 4 (Syncopation)

The traditional way of teaching counterpoint puts syncopation in its own category.

FIG. 2.4. Species 4

Species 5 (Mixture)

Also called "florid counterpoint," species 5 puts it all together—mixes it up—like in real music.

FIG. 2.5. Species 5

As mentioned, species counterpoint is the traditional approach to teaching counterpoint. This book departs from that pedagogy by applying traditional counterpoint techniques to contemporary musical styles. In particular, while the pitch and rhythmic idioms of various styles differ, there is a relevancy across styles regarding the rhythmic "give and take" between voices. From the basic 1:1 ratio in species one to polyrhythms and asymmetrical rhythmic combinations, an awareness of and ability to manipulate independent and interrelated rhythmic patterns directly impacts the music's effectiveness. The rhythmic ratios from the species table generally can be applied to any style of contrapuntal music where the independent melodic lines move back and forth from the foreground to the background of a polyphonic texture. Effectively using these ratios by trading the faster and slower rhythms and rhythmic patterns between voices creates a natural fluidity and an effective fabric of counterpoint.

"Tappster, Drynker" Rhythmic Ratios

Let's look at the rhythmic ratios in the contrapuntal drinking song, "Tappster, Drynker," from the Renaissance era. This song is about a bunch of people in a tavern singing for more ale—a common theme that has been a popular subject for songs throughout the ages and even today.[2]

Notice that there are three separate voices in this music, each one with its own melody and all three voices working harmoniously together. Follow the direction of the note stems in the bass staff to indicate tenor (note stems up) and bass (note stems down) voices. Available recordings include "Winter and Wassail: Tappster, Drynker," anonymous, *Thys Yool: A Medieval Christmas*; Martin Best Ensemble, Nimbus Records (1992). Here are the lyrics (Middle English):

> *Drynker, fyll another ale,*
> *Anonn God sende us good sale.*
> *Avale the stake, avale,*
> *here is good ale y founde.*
> *Drynke to me and y to the*
> *and lette the cuppe goe rounde.*

---

2   Music notation evolved through the centuries, and in the fifteenth century when the "Tappster, Drynker" song was written, the noteheads were different shapes indicating different durations. The notation used here is modern notation.

Tappster, Drynker

English Part Song, c. 1475

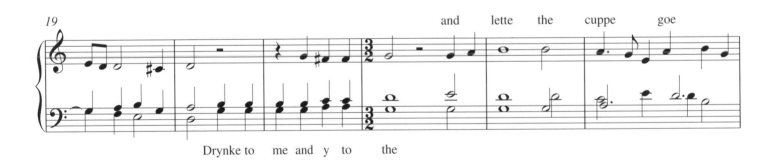

FIG. 2.6. "Tappster, Drynker"

ACTIVITY 2.1. NAME THE RHYTHMIC RATIOS

Identify the rhythmic ratios between each pair of voices by answering the following questions.

FIG. 2.7. Activity 2.1. "Tappster, Drynker" (Excerpt)

1. The majority of ratios in this excerpt are:

   a. 1:1

   b. 2:1

   c. 3:1

   d. syncopation

2. Where is the first occurrence of the 2:1 ratio?

   a. measure 4, beat 3, between the treble and middle voice

   b. measure 6, beats 3–4, between the treble/middle voices and the bass voice

   c. measure 8, beats 1–2, between the treble/middle voices and the bass voice

   d. measure 10, beat 3, between the treble/bass voices and the middle voice

3. Where does the first instance of syncopation occur?

   a. measure 4, beat 3, between the treble and middle voice

   b. measure 8, beat 4 to measure 9, beat 1, between the middle/bass voices and the treble voice

    c. measure 9, beat 4 to measure 10, beat 1, between the treble/bass voices and the middle voice

    d. measure 10, beats 3–4, between the middle/bass voices and the treble voice

4. Where does the last instance of syncopation occur in this excerpt?

    a. measure 4, beat 3, between the treble and middle voice

    b. measure 8, beat 4 to measure 9, beat 1, between the treble/middle voices and the bass voice

    c. measure 9, beat 4 to measure 10, beat 1, between the treble/bass voices and the middle voice

    d. measure 10, beats 3–4, between the middle/bass voices and the treble voice

Answers are at the end of this chapter.

WRITING TWO-VOICE COUNTERPOINT

How are multiple voices created to make a polyphonic texture? Historically, composers were hired, most often by the Church or royalty, to write a new melody over an older, pre-existing melody that was familiar to many people. The new music was often created to celebrate a birthday, anniversary, wedding, or religious event. The novelty of the new melody, presented with the familiarity of a pre-existing melody, allowed the listener to enjoy something new along with the reassurance of what is already recognized. We see this technique used in today's contemporary art of sampling. Think of the many hits of today that are built from a snippet of yesterday's hits. Counterpoint results when the sampling takes a musical line or segment of texture that continues for more than a few seconds and adds a new musical line to that original texture.

In counterpoint, the addition of this new voice is called the "counterpoint line." That is, an extra voice is added as a "counter-point" to a pre-existing melody. While the new melody is called the counterpoint, the pre-existing melody, or the "fixed song," is called cantus firmus (abbreviated CF), from the Latin: *cantus* (song) and *firmus* (fixed). The "counter-point" refers to the note (point) from the original melody being presented against another note or notes (Latin: *contra punctus*) from the newly created melody.

This practice was a formalization of the common practice, dating back even further in music history, of improvising over a given melody, bass line, rhythmic pattern, or chord progression. Improvisation operated in the same way back then as it does today in popular music like blues, jazz, Latin, and bluegrass.

For example, let's take a basic blues bass line as the *cantus firmus* and add a treble line, as if improvised, but in this case written out, to be the new melody or *counterpoint.*

FIG. 2.8. Blues Example (Excerpt)

Let's look more closely at the ratios, intervals, and other analysis techniques that will help us write effective counterpoint. Here is the blues excerpt with the rhythmic ratios and intervals identified.

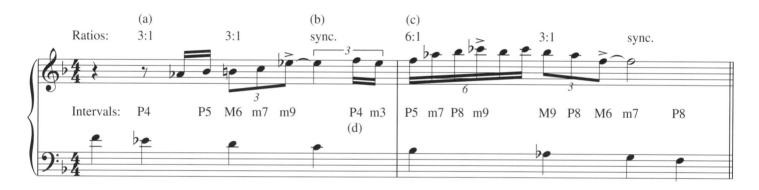

FIG. 2.9. Blues Example with Analysis

Note:

(a) Ratios do not account for rests. In this case, the first eighth rest of beat 2 is considered a silent "note."

(b) The syncopation category is used when notes are tied over the beat or a stronger portion of the beat, and then articulations occur off the beat.

(c) While 6:1 is not a traditional ratio measurement, we can clearly see that there are six notes in the treble to the one note in the bass.

(d) The remaining intervals, except for the ninths, are identified as simple intervals instead of compound intervals.

MELODIC GESTURES: PHRASES

Did you notice how the counterpoint line in the blues excerpt sounded like a complete thought? It is a melodic gesture with a beginning, middle, and end. This is called a musical *phrase*. Phrases can be graceful, as in the melodic contours of this example, or angular and irregular; they can be short and quick or slow and long and anything in between. Phrases can be in many shapes and sizes and are created by assembling several *motives*.

- Several notes can be grouped together to create a motive. A motive is the smallest structural unit in music composition. We will learn more about motives in chapter 3.

- Several motives can be grouped together in several measures.

- Several measures—often four measures, but not always—can be grouped together to form a melodic gesture, or phrase.

- Phrases often work in pairs, multiple pairs, and/or larger groups of phrases to make larger sections of music.

Consider the phrase much like the physical gesture of sweeping your hand in an arc. It has a single, overall shape that contains a beginning, middle, and end. Here are two more examples.

This phrase sounds sad, and the notes move forward lyrically, as in a ballad.

Audio 10

FIG. 2.10. Sad Phrase. (Audio without lyrics.)

This second phrase sounds silly and the notes move in a more choppy, animated manner.

FIG. 2.11. Silly Phrase. (Audio without lyrics.)

Just as one can make different types of physical gestures (lyrical arm swings vs. choppy hand motions), phrases can express many different types of musical motion.

While phrases can be of any length, these two phrases are both four measures long. This is the most frequent phrase length found in many different styles of music. However, phrases of other lengths are often preferable for many reasons, including lyrics, tempo, and chord changes.

CALL-AND-RESPONSE PHRASE PAIRS

Many pieces of music, including contrapuntal compositions, are put together as a series of phrases, and often the phrases are related to each other in a call-and-response relationship within individual sections.

For example, in many forms of popular music, there is often a call-and-response relationship between the first two phrases in the A section.

In this example, do you see the call and response? The first phrase after the introduction, in measures 5–8, is the call. The second phrase, the response (or answer) is in measures 9–11.

Audio 11

You Are the Bright Light in My Night

FIG. 2.12. Introduction and Call-and-Response Phrases

Let's add a counterpoint to this pre-existing melody:

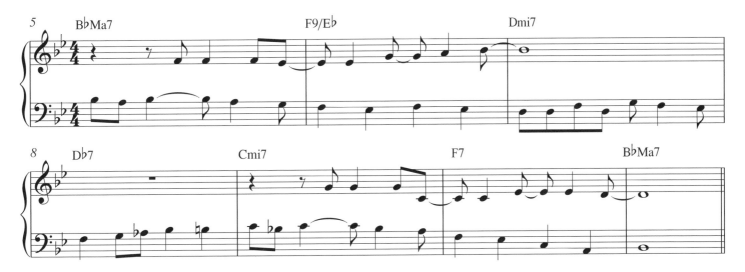

FIG. 2.13. Call-and-Response Phrases with Added Counterpoint Line

While the call-and-response melodic gestures are still clearly heard, the added line helps move the music forward by connecting the two phrases. This new counterpoint line also sounds like a melodic bass line; counterpoint helps us write effective arrangements, too! An excellent bass player often plays lines that can stand on their own as independent melodies, and so those lines would qualify as counterpoint. It's all around us: listen and you will hear polyphonic textures in places you never expected to hear them before.

"MENUET" BY ÉLISABETH JACQUET DE LA GUERRE FROM THE *SUITE NO. 4 IN F MAJOR*

Returning to the "golden age" of counterpoint, the Baroque era, this "Menuet" is a three-voice contrapuntal composition, as was "Tappster, Drynker" (although "Tappster, Drynker" was from the earlier Renaissance era). In the "Menuet," the third voice enters in the second measure of the B section. Note that the tenor quarter rest shows the entrance of the third voice (tenor and bass voices are on the same staff). Play through this piece yourself and/or you can listen to multiple available recordings including *Élisabeth-Claude Jacquet de La Guerre: Harpsichord Suites Nos. 1-6*; Elizabeth Farr, Naxos Records.

Menuet
from *Suite 4 in F Major*

Élisabeth Jacquet de La Guerre

FIG. 2.14. "Menuet" from *Suite No. 4 in F Major* by Élisabeth Jacquet de La Guerre

The piece opens with a three-note motive beginning on A and again, starting on F, in measure 2. The second half of the phrase uses eighth notes in the treble voice that increases the forward drive to the end of the phrase at measure 4 beat 3.

FIG. 2.15. Motive, Measures, and Phrase in the "Menuet"

In more traditional sounding counterpoint, like this piece, you will usually find only consonant intervals during 1:1 ratio, and dissonant intervals are found in other ratios as specific non-chord tones.

Can you hear the ending of each melodic gesture in the call-and-response phrases of the A section? Each phrase's ending is called a *cadence*. All phrases conclude with a cadence marking the end of the melodic gesture. For phrase pairs, the second cadence will sound more conclusive than the first. In classical music, the first phrase (the "call") is called "antecedent" (that which comes before) and the second phrase (the "response") is called "consequent" (that which comes afterwards).

CADENCES

The harmonic element of most cadences is the last two chords of the phrase. The following table lists some basic cadences with their names, abbreviations, and brief descriptions.

ABBREVIATIONS	CADENCE NAME	BRIEF DESCRIPTION
PAC	Perfect Authentic Cadence	Dominant to tonic chords with the tonic scale degree in the treble and both chords with the root in the bass.
IAC	Imperfect Authentic Cadence	Dominant to tonic chords with any of the following variations: the third or fifth scale degree may be in the treble of the tonic chord; either chord can be voiced with the third in the bass; the leading tone chord can be substituted for the dominant chord.
PC	Plagal Cadence	Subdominant to tonic chords, as often found in the "Amen" cadence at the end of church hymns.
DC	Deceptive Cadence	Dominant to submediant (VI) chords. It "deceives" the listener who expects the tonic chord to follow the dominant as in the authentic cadences.
HC	Half Cadence	The phrase ends on the dominant chord. Often the cadence of choice for the first phrase of a phrase pair. It sounds open, as if asking a question.

FIG. 2.16. Cadence Table

In the A Section of the "Menuet," both phrases end with an imperfect authentic cadence. So why does the second phrase sound more conclusive? There are two reasons for this effect. First, there is very little rhythmic break in the melody between phrases 1 and 2. The first phrase ends on measure 4, beat 3, and the second phrase begins on measure 5, beat 1. The quarter note articulations continue from one phrase to the next. Second, phrase 1's harmonic motion moves from dominant to tonic at the downbeat of measure 4, but the melodic motion continues to beat 3, a weak beat; whereas, the response phrase's melodic motion ends on measure 8, beat 1: the downbeat. All motion stops at the downbeat of measure 8. Both the melodic gesture and the harmonic implications have come to a halt. This is why the second cadence, while being the same type as the first, sounds more conclusive.

Jacquet de La Guerre's "Menuet" contains two phrases in the A section (four measures each) and two more phrases in the B section (six measures each). The same rhythmic relationship between the phrases in the A section is found between the phrases in the B section. Review the harmonic analysis in figure 2.19. The circled notes are the non-chord tones and should not be included in identifying the harmonic implications.

FIGURED BASS

The Arabic numbers next to the Roman numerals in the "Menuet" analysis on page 30 show the chord's voicing. Any member of a chord can be in the bass, and the other chord members above the bass note are described by the Arabic number indicating the interval they create with that bass note. The following table summarizes these figured bass numbers (also called inversion symbols and bass positioning symbols).

BASS NOTE	➡	ROOT	THIRD	FIFTH	SEVENTH
Triads	Full Listing	5 3	6 3	8 6 4	N/A
	Shorthand	(blank)	6	6 4	N/A
Seventh Chords	Full Listing	7 5 3	6 5 3	6 4 3	6 4 2
	Shorthand	7	6 5	4 3	4 2
Inversion Name		Root Position	First Inversion	Second Inversion	Third Inversion

FIG. 2.17. Figured Bass Table

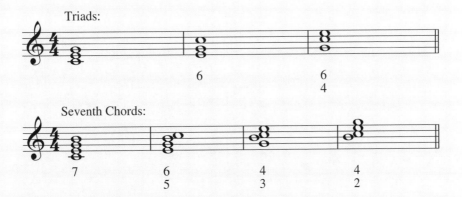

FIG. 2.18. Musical Example of Figured Bass Symbols

The notes for any voicing can be *closed*, as in these examples—that is, as close together as possible, or they can be *open*, spread out over several octaves and in any order (above the bass note).

Menuet
from *Suite 4 in F Major*

Élisabeth Jacquet de La Guerre

FIG. 2.19. Analysis of "Menuet"

Contrapuntal music combines various rhythmic ratios between voices. While the "Menuet" is composed mostly of 1:1 and 2:1 ratios, notice also the ratio 3:1 in measure 3, beats 1–2; the 4:1 ratio occurs in measures 4, 12, and 18, beats 1–2; and syncopations, as defined by the species system, occur in measures 10 and 16.

BEAUTIFUL OHIO

And now for something more contemporary. This is the official song for the state of Ohio, U.S., and has the call-and-response phrase pairs we saw in the "Bright Light" and "Menuet" tunes. Many arrangements and recordings of this song are available both as the originally scored waltz (big band versions: Tommy Dorsey, Ralph Marterie) and as a march for the Ohio State Marching Band, too. Listen or play through this piece and hear the call-and-response phrase pairs.

Beautiful Ohio

Ballard MacDonald

Robert A. King

FIG. 2.20. "Beautiful Ohio"

Let's add a bass line that is melodic so that the two voices work together in a contrapuntal texture. Keeping the following general principles in mind when writing counterpoint will help establish and maintain melodic independence.

The rhythmic "give and take" between voices is maximized. If the pre-existing melody has a lot of notes, the counterpoint line sometimes hangs back with rests and slower moving notes.

Many melodies are composed primarily of stepwise motion. Use leaps for excitement and contrast.

You may notice a sweetness or conservative sound to the note choices. This is achieved by emphasizing the chord tones and consonant intervals (octaves, fifths, thirds, and sixths). These notes are placed on the stronger beats, and the in-between notes (the non-chord tones) are on the weaker beats or portions of the beat.

Direction of line: when the two voices move in opposite directions there is an increased urgency in the forward motion of the music. This is called *contrary motion*. When moving in the same direction, there is more of a peaceful feel to the motion. This is called *parallel motion* (when both voices are moving in the same direction by the same interval) or *similar motion* (when both voices are moving in the same direction but by different intervals). Be careful: If the counterpoint voice moves in parallel motion with the pre-existing melody—for example, in parallel thirds for the whole time—then it will sound like the melody is being harmonized and the independence of the counterpoint voice will be lost.

Audio 12

FIG. 2.21. "Beautiful Ohio" in Two-Voice Counterpoint

ACTIVITY 2.2. WRITING YOUR OWN COUNTERPOINT

Find your own favorite tune, analyze the phrases and harmonic implications, and then create your own counterpoint line to make a contrapuntal texture. For extra practice, also identify all intervals, ratios, and phrases.

SUMMARY

Now you know how to identify and use various rhythmic ratios in writing your own contrapuntal music. We examined how measures work together to form phrases. The call-and-response relationship within a pair of phrases occurs when the second cadence is more conclusive than the first. This can be done by choosing different types of cadences and/or by their rhythmic placement as in the Jacquet "Menuet." Grouping phrases in call-and-response pairs is one way of creating more effective sections of music. We saw how these elements were used in a Renaissance drinking song, a Baroque minuet, a jazz standard, and a contemporary pop piece. You applied all of this in writing your own counterpoint line above or below a favorite melody of your own choosing.

ACTIVITY ANSWERS

Activity 2.1

1, a; 2, c; 3, b; 4, d

CHAPTER 3

Motivic Manipulation

A *motive*, also called a "motif," is a small musical idea used to create larger segments of music. In chapter 2, we noticed that several motives work together to create a phrase. In this chapter, we will investigate how the motive is manipulated to create and develop musical themes.

A motive can be modified in many ways, including stretching its length, restating it at other pitch levels, and even turning it upside down. Most of the examples given here will be for a single voice. Exercises in motivic manipulation for a single voice isolate the techniques and prepare one to apply these skills to imitative counterpoint for multiple voices, which we will explore in subsequent chapters.

WHAT IS A MOTIVE?

The Medieval Latin word for motive, *motivus*, means serving to move or inspire. A motive is a motivating idea in music. It can be melodic, harmonic, timbral, and/or rhythmic. It is an important part of a theme, and is often combined with other corroborating motives within a theme.

Activity 3.1. Listen

The following four compositions have memorable motives (see excerpts in figures 3.1 through figure 3.4). While listening to the suggested recordings, notice restatements and variations of the motives.

Johann Sebastian Bach, Ein musikalisches Opfer, BWV1079 – Movement 1: Ricercare a 3

This motive is the first part of a longer theme that was presented to Bach in 1747 as a challenge to test his genius. Bach, never one to be undone by a challenge, *improvised* a three-voice fugue on the spot! He went on to develop the theme in various canonic puzzles, as a trio sonata, and the pièce de résistance: a six-voice fugue. Available recordings include *Bach: Organ Miniatures*; Christopher Herrick, Hyperion Records Ltd, London (1990).

FIG. 3.1. "1. Ricercare a 3" from *Ein musikalisches Opfer*, BWV1079 by J.S. Bach, Measures 1–3

Ludwig van Beethoven, Symphony No. 5, Movement 1

One of the most famous pieces of all time is Beethoven's "Fifth." The powerful motive at the beginning of the first movement has inspired many composers, past and present, for over two hundred years since Beethoven composed it. Walter Murphy's famous disco hit "A Fifth of Beethoven" (1976) may be the most well known contemporary reinterpretation, but there are also contemporary samplings of this music by hip-hop artists and dance DJs. Original recordings available include *Symphony No. 3 & No. 5*; Philharmonic Promenade Orchestra of London, Sir Adrian Boult, Artemis-Vanguard (1965).

FIG. 3.2. "1. Allegro con brio" from *Symphony No. 5* by Ludwig van Beethoven, Measures 1–2

Hector-Louis Berlioz, Symphonie Fantastique," Op.14, "Rêveries–Passions"

Berlioz, who considered Beethoven the greatest composer of all time, wrote *Symphonie Fantastique* (1830) to describe his passion for a beautiful actress named Harriet Smithson, whom he pursued and then married. This motive, near the beginning of the first movement, is a short part of a much longer theme Berlioz called the *idée fixe*— the object of fixation, that is, his obsession for the love of his life. Available recordings include *Symphonie Fantastique: episode de la vie d'un artiste*; Orchestre Philharmonique des Pays de Loire, Fioretti (1994).

FIG. 3.3. "Rêveries–Passions" from *Symphonie Fantastique, Op.14* by Hector-Louis Berlioz, Measures 3–4

Muzio Clementi, Piano Sonata in F-Sharp Minor, Op. 26, No. 2, Movement 1

Clementi was born almost twenty years before Beethoven, whom he met when both were in Vienna. While Clementi was well known on the European continent, he spent most of his life in England where he was also active as a music publisher and piano builder. Figure 3.4 presents the opening motive for this sonata. It is principal to the first theme and used extensively throughout the movement. Available recordings include *Horowitz Plays Clementi*; Vladimir Horowitz, RCA Records (1989).

FIG. 3.4. "I. Allegro con espressione" from *Piano Sonata in F-Sharp Minor*, Op. 26, No. 2 by Muzio Clementi, Measures 1–2

Activity 3.1 Finding Motives in Popular Songs

Do you have a favorite piece of music that has a distinct motive? Whether you select another piece or one of the examples above, describe the motive and name a few reasons why you like it.

For example, here is the A section from a jazz melody. The four-note motive is interesting because it sounds very different as it moves up in pitch, recurs under different harmonies, and is transformed by adjusting intervals and using only part of the motive.

Audio 13

Befuddled

FIG. 3.5. Jazz Melody, A Section

HOW TO USE A MOTIVE AS A GENERATING DEVICE

Turn it upside down, backwards, stretch it, squeeze it. It's fun, it's a MOTIVE!

Sequence

Let's look again at this motive from Bach's 1. *Ricercare a 3*:

FIG. 3.6. *Ricercare a 3*, Measures 1–3

The alto voice plays this part of the theme again at measure 10. This time in half notes beginning on "G" instead of "C."

FIG. 3.7. "Ricercare a 3" Measure 10

When a motive is repeated but begins at a different pitch, it is called a *sequence*.

Real Sequence

If the repetition is exactly the same—that is, all the notes are the same distance apart from each other (intervals) as they were in the original version, then that sequence is said to be "real." Using a real sequence can be very helpful when moving from one key to another (modulation).

Tonal Sequence

Sometimes one or more of the intervals has been adjusted. Most often this is done to stay diatonic (in the key), rather than to modulate. This type of sequence is called "tonal."

The sequence may be the most frequent way that a motive is manipulated.

Activity 3.2. Real vs. Tonal Sequences

Using Bach's motive from the *Ricercare*, answer the following questions:

Original Motive

FIG. 3.8. Original Motive, Measures 1–3

    1. Is this sequence tonal or real?

    2. Which note changed?

FIG. 3.9. Measures 10–12

Explanation: The sequence has been lowered a fourth except for the third note which has dropped a fifth. This is a tonal sequence because (at least) one of the notes has been changed. Another way of describing this is that one of the intervals has changed, that is, the intervallic distance between the second and third notes has *diminuted* (shortened) from a third (in measures 1–2) to a second (in measures 10–11).

    3. This same motive (see figure 3.9) recurs again in measures 46–48 (see figure 3.10), also as a sequence beginning on G. Compare figures 3.9 and 3.10. Are they the same?

    4. Which note has changed from figure 3.9 to figure 3.10?

    5. Compare figure 3.10 to figure 3.8. Is the sequence in figure 3.10 tonal or real?

FIG. 3.10. Measures 46–48

Explanation: Compared to the original sequence in m. 1, all the notes have been lowered by a fourth (including the third note).

Measure 1

Measure 46

FIG. 3.11. Compare Measures 1–3 to Measures 46–48

In a real sequence, all of the intervals remain the same. In measure 46, all the intervals are the same as they were in measure 1, so this is a real sequence. The music is now in G minor, no longer in C minor.

MORE MOTIVE MANIPULATIONS
Rhythmic Augmentation

The augmentation of a motive uses a rhythmic permutation to "augment" the length of the motive. The most frequent usage is to make each note twice as long.

Here's the original Clementi motive:

FIG. 3.12. Clementi Motive

Here's the Clementi motive with rhythmic augmentation:

FIG. 3.13. Clementi with Rhythmic Augmentation

Diminution

Another rhythmic permutation is to "diminish" the length of the motive. Here's the motive from Bach's "Ricercare."

FIG. 3.14. "Ricercare" Motive, Original Version

Here is the same motive with diminution.

FIG. 3.15. "Ricercare" Motive with Rhythmic Diminution

CHANGING THINGS AROUND
Changing or Adding Notes

When does a dog turn into a chicken? You can have a black dog, a white dog, a speckled dog, or a tan dog; they are all dogs. But if you make too many changes then it may not be recognizable as a dog anymore!

It is the same with motives. You can add a note here or there, or change a note (as in the difference between a real and a tonal sequence) here or there. But if you make too many changes it will lose connection to the original motive.

Below is the Bach motive with a few changes that work.

- Filling in the scale degrees between chord members (which remain on the beat, in the motive) can be an effective way to develop a motive.

FIG. 3.16. "Ricercare" Motive with Additional Notes

- Change a note to support diatonic harmony:

FIG. 3.17. "Ricercare" Motive on G (Tonal Sequence) with a Changed Note

Change of Mode

Jazz and other popular styles of music are often based on different modes. There are, for example, modes derived from the major scale (Ionian, Dorian, Phrygian, Lydian, Mixolydian, Aeolian, and Locrian) and those from the melodic minor scale (jazz minor, Dorian ♭9, Lydian augmented, Lydian dominant, Mixolydian ♭6, Semilocrian, Superlocrian). There are also alternative scales in both jazz and contemporary classical, for example: pentatonic, whole tone, and octatonic (also called symmetrical diminished scales). Scales and modes other than the traditional major and minor configurations are often used inside a tonal or modal framework to express varying levels of brightness and darkness and are appropriate for various chords.

In traditional classical music (also called the common practice period ca. 1750–1900), tonality is the harmonic framework in which the music occurs. Within this limitation, the term "mode" only refers to the color changes between a major scale and the minor scale that starts on the same note—that is, the parallel minor (e.g., C major and C minor). Returning to Berlioz' *Symphonie Fantastique*, the opening motive excerpted before (and below) occurs after a full voicing of the C minor chord and the motive itself is in C minor.

FIG. 3.18. Berlioz Motive in C Minor, Measures 3–4

When the full theme occurs in the flute, the key has changed to C major and this motive, occurring near the middle part of the theme, is stated in rhythmic augmentation with some slight durational variations and is clearly in C major.

FIG. 3.19. Berlioz Motive in C Major, Measures 90–94

The traditional classical term for this, "change of mode," only refers to the shift from happy to sad with the same tonic note—for example, from C major to C minor; or from sad to happy, as in going from B minor to B major.

Audio 14

In jazz, mode change offers many other color modifications. Here's an originally happy melody in C major gradually descending into the darkness of C Locrian.

C Phrygian

C Locrian

FIG. 3.20. Motivic Manipulation by Changing Modes in Jazz

INVERSION AND RETROGRADE
Inversion

Inversion is sometimes called "contrary motion," or "upside down." The notes go in the opposite direction but maintain the same (intervallic) distance from each other.

For example, if an interval in the original motive went down a third, at that same place in the inversion, that interval would go up a third.

Listen to (or play) Bach's "Invention No. 1 in C Major." Available recordings include *Bach: Inventions, Sinfonia & Duets*; Peter Serkin, piano, BMG Entertainment (1997).

Here's the original motive, beginning on C, in measure 1:

FIG. 3.21. Bach, "Invention No. 1," Measure 1

Here's the inverted version, beginning on A, in measure 3:

FIG. 3.22. Bach, "Invention No. 1," Measure 3

Bach's "Invention No. 1" then goes on and sequences the inverted form four times.

FIG. 3.23. Bach, "Invention No. 1," Measures 3–4

Retrograde

Retrograde means going backwards. The last note becomes the first and so on and so forth until the first is the last. Some motives are not well suited for retrograde treatment. However, the Bach "Ricercare a 3" motive works quite well backwards.

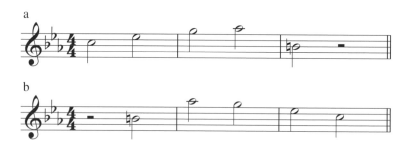

FIG. 3.24. Bach, "Ricercare a 3" (a) Original Motive, (b) Retrograde

Activity 3.3. Matching Manipulations

Here is a motive (first example on audio 15).

FIG. 3.25. Motive for Activity 3.3

Match the correct term with the motivic manipulation shown:

Audio 15

change of mode   diminution   retrograde   inversion

augmentation   addition of notes   sequence

1.

2.

3.

4.

5.

6.

7.

FIG. 3.26. Activity 3.3

Answers are at the end of the chapter.

Activity 3.4. Applying Motivic Manipulations

Manipulate the motive in figure 3.27 in three different ways, as a:

1. sequence
2. inversion
3. retrograde

FIG. 3.27. Motive for Activity 3.4

DIGGING IN DEEPER

Another way of manipulating a motive is to use just part of it. This is called *fragmentation*:

- Using only a part of a motive, after stating the full motive, can extend the length of a musical idea or phrase.

- Often this fragment is sequenced and repeated more than once.

- This technique is especially effective when approaching the end of a phrase as it increases urgency for the drive to the end (cadence).

The gradual fragmentation of the eight-note motive of Theme 2 from the first movement of Beethoven's *Fifth Symphony* demonstrates this motivic manipulation technique. The eight notes are stated, all in quarter notes, in measures 63–66 and then repeated twice, in complete form. Measures 75–78 fragment the motive into two groups of four (first group related to the middle of the original motive) and yet retain the single unit of eight notes through their motivic relationship to each other. The following sequence of these eight notes is up a third in measures 79–82. The four-note motivic relationship is maintained: two ascending steps and a descending step followed by a retrograde of those notes down a step. The eight-note unit is now clearly heard as two parts of four notes each. The fragmentation is carried even further in measures 83–84 where only the first of the two four-note units is stated and then immediately repeated four more times. The final fragmentation at this point is to reduce the motive to three notes up to the half cadence at measure 94. We can summarize Beethoven's use of motivic fragmentation in this example by the grouping of notes as eight, then four plus four, then four, and then three.

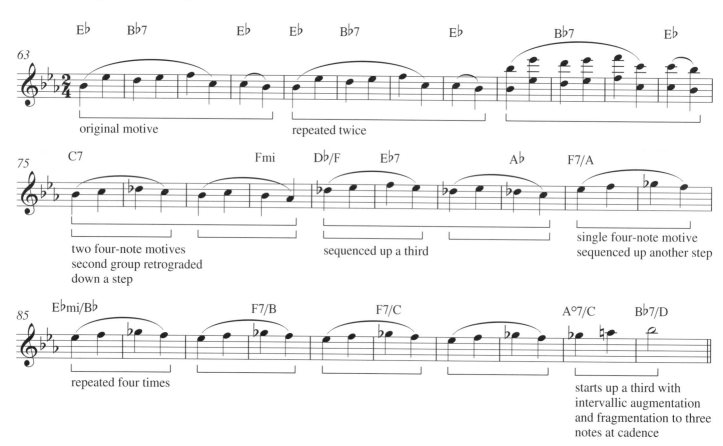

FIG. 3.28. Beethoven, *Fifth Symphony*, "1. Allegro con brio" Theme 2, Measures 63–94

Repetition

Repetition of a motive, phrase, or musical section is another way to extend the music. This may be considered a manipulation, in that the same idea is repeated at a different place in time. But because there is no change to the motive itself, it is a temporal manipulation, rather than a manipulation of pitches and/or rhythms.

The "Entrance Hymn for the Emperor" theme, a Chinese melody from around 1000 CE, uses repetition and some motivic manipulation. In figure 3.29 measures 3–6 repeat in measures 7–10. Then measures 11–14 repeat again but this time with rhythmic diminution, then augmentation, and then some intervallic variation. Available recordings include Ensemble Renaissance, *Marco Polo–The Journey*, Ensemble Renaissance (2014).

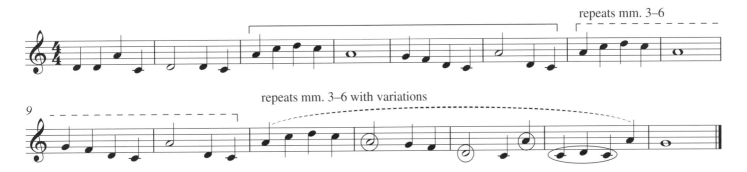

FIG. 3.29. "Entrance Hymn to the Emperor"

REVIEW

We have looked at the following motivic manipulations:

- Sequences: real and tonal
- Rhythmic: diminution and augmentation
- Changing and/or adding notes
- Change of mode
- Inversion
- Retrograde
- Fragmentation
- Repetition

UNCOVERING MOTIVES

Motivic manipulation is sometimes very clear to hear and see. This is often the case when a two-measure motive is immediately sequenced (or a four-measure phrase as in the beginnings of many U.S. television series' theme songs from the 1970s and 1980s). Other times, it is more challenging to find the connection between the motivic manipulations and the original. Think about the examples in this chapter. Which manipulations were easy to find? Which ones were not as easy to find?

In these next two examples, you will find sequencing, repetition, inversion, retrograde, rhythmic diminution and augmentation, and fragmentation.

Festa and "La Spagna No. 36"

Composers and improvisers have used motivic manipulation techniques for many centuries. About 500 years ago, and continuing for several centuries after that, a particular basse danse melody called "La Spagna" (it was also known under other names) was often used as a slow moving cantus firmus for added counterpoint.

In earlier usage, it was often used for improvisation—that is, the added contrapuntal line was played, rather than being written down. When "La Spagna" regained popularity in the seventeenth century it was used as the cantus firmus to which composers added counterpoint, written down, for multiple voices.

FIG. 3.30. "La Spagna" Basse Danse

Many composers wrote contrapuntal elaborations on top of "La Spagna," and we can only speculate how many hundreds of performers improvised on it. One of the more famous composers who used it was Constanzo Festa, a sixteenth century papal singer. He wrote 120 compositions over this cantus firmus, and we know this because there are letters from him petitioning a well-known publisher to print his compositions!

Festa's compositions straddle the Medieval and Renaissance periods, so the particular setting we will look at is mostly modal rather than tonal. You will hear phrases and cadential gestures, but the latter will be in stepwise motion moving away from each other with a change in the rhythm. This "La Spagna" setting by Festa is mostly in D Dorian with some small portions in D Aeolian. The score in figure 3.31 has added motivic analysis. Listen to the counterpoint and then listen again while reading the annotations on the score.

La Spagna
Counterpoint 36 from Bologna C36

Constanzo Festa

FIG. 3.31. Excerpt from "Counterpoint No. 36" from *Bologna Manuscript 36*. Attributed to Festa, with added motivic analysis.

"Befuddled," Section A

What about the motivic manipulations in that jazz tune we looked at earlier in this chapter? What are the motivic segments of that melody and how do those segments relate to each other?

Motivic manipulation builds on familiarity and novelty. When a melodic segment sounds similar enough to remind one of the music that came before, and yet has something new enough to spark continued interest in listening, then the line may be considered effective. In "Befuddled," see figure 3.32, the four-note motive brings change with each reiteration until it becomes something totally new. However, because the new elements are gradually introduced, the melody gently leads the listener into new terrain. While some elements are becoming something totally new, other elements are remaining constant, anchoring the listener. Which pitch or rhythmic elements within the motive remain constant and which ones change? The following points refer each restatement of the motive to the corresponding numbered items in the score.

1. The original motive: up a step, down two steps.

2. The distance between the second and third notes has been stretched to a third; rhythm and placement in the measure is the same.

3. The stretched distance between the second and the third notes is maintained and a new stretch of a third occurs between the third and fourth notes. The rhythm of articulations is maintained, but the fourth note is now a quarter note instead of a half note.

4. This motive enters two beats early. The last note of the previous motive was cut in half and the first note of this motive is missing. The new stretching is now a fourth instead of a third. All three manipulations in this fourth statement of the motive (the early entry, skipping the first note, and stretching to a tritone instead of a third) contribute to the novelty of the line. The listener's curiosity is piqued and the music drives forward with more urgency as the fragmentation has begun.

5. The three-note version occurs again although the last note is restored to its half note duration.

6. The note grouping is reduced again, this time to two notes. The rhythmic placement and step-wise relationship is a reminder of the first two notes (pick-up to measure 1).

7. The isolation of the ascending step is now extended to six steps and prepares for the closing cadence.

One added element that brings cohesion to this melody is the use of register. At the bottom of the register there is a continual return to the lowest pitch of D with each reiteration of the motive in measures 1–4. The other registral element that contributes to the forward motion and urgency of the melody is the ever-expanding upper edge of the register. As the motive recurs in measures 1–4, the highest pitch ascends from F♯ to G to A to A♯ to B.

Befuddled

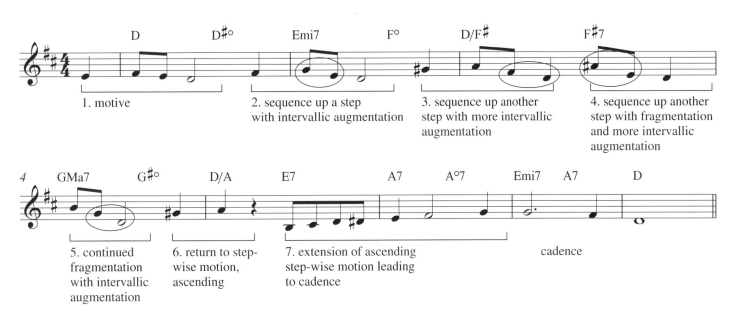

FIG. 3.32. Jazz Melody, A Section, with Added Motivic Analysis

Activity 3.4. Creating Your Own Counterpoint Using Motivic Manipulations

Rewrite these last thirteen measures of the "La Spagna" using a grand staff, and add your own counterpoint in the treble line (see figure 3.33). Regarding consonance and dissonance: you do not need to restrict yourself to the regulations of modal (or tonal) counterpoint: be creative while selecting the motivic manipulations that work well together as you create phrases. Don't forget the power of rhythmic definition and that you can use rests, too. Write a brief analysis narrative describing your original motive and the motivic manipulations you employed.

FIG. 3.33. Write Your Own Counterpoint, Last Thirteen Measures of "La Spagna"

SUMMARY

In this chapter, we looked at several motives from famous compositions in the Baroque, Classical, Romantic, and jazz style periods, as well as an ancient Chinese royal theme. We examined motives and demonstrated how they could be manipulated. You practiced identifying the following types of motivic manipulations: inversion (upside down), retrograde (backwards), rhythmic augmentation and diminution (stretch or squeeze), sequence (restate it at different pitch levels), modal interchange, fragmentation, repetition, and addition, subtraction, and adjustment of notes. You learned how to manipulate motives, and you created your own imitative counterpoint for the "La Spagna" cantus firmus using motivic manipulation.

ACTIVITY ANSWERS

Activity 3.2 Answers

1. tonal, 2. the third note, 3. no, 4. the third note, 5. real

Activity 3.3 Answers

1. inversion, 2. addition of notes, 3. sequence, 4. retrograde, 5. change of mode, 6. augmentation, 7. diminution

CHAPTER 4

Canon

In this chapter, we will look at the *canon*, one specific type of imitative counterpoint. We will examine several canonic pieces including "Sumer Is Icumen In," one of the earliest notated examples of a canon, as well as other traditional and contemporary pieces, and you will learn how to write a simple canon at the octave.

WHAT IS A CANON?

"Canon" means rule, or law, and in music, the simple canon uses a very strict rule to define itself. Canons are like the children's game "Follow the Leader" where the leader makes a move and the follower must do what the leader does, but afterwards, rather than simultaneously. In addition, in canon, the follower begins imitating the leader while the leader is still singing.

In a canon there are at least two voices—a leader and a follower. The follower voice sings the same music as the leader voice but begins after the leader has started but before the leader stops. When the follower voice sings exactly the same as the leader voice, it is called a *strict canon*, but when the follower voice makes a minor adjustment or two, it is called a *free canon*. Canons can also be written for three, four, eight, twelve—any number of voices.

One of the simplest forms of a canon is the *round*. Rounds are found in many folk traditions and children's songs. For example, in the traditonal French favorite, "Frère Jacques," (figure 4.1, English version), the numbers above the staff indicate that this round is for four voices. Each number tells the corresponding follower voice (voices 2 to 4) when to begin singing the melody in relation to the leader (1) voice.

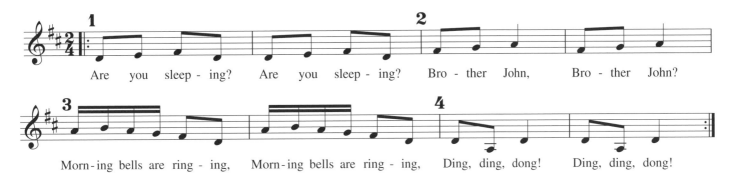

FIG. 4.1. "Frère Jacques" Round

Audio 17

Figure 4.2 shows the round written out for two voices using the second vocal entrance of the round for the follower voice. A round is called an "infinite canon," because as soon as you get to the end, you go back to the beginning. It could go on and on forever!

FIG. 4.2. "Frère Jacques" as an Infinite Canon for Two Voices

The follower voice begins with the downbeat of measure 3 (see the first full-sized note in the bass voice), an octave below the leader voice. The distance between the first note of the leader voice and the first note of the follower voice defines the interval of the canon, in this case: the octave. This is an infinite canon at the octave.

Consider the harmonic implications of this "Frère Jacques" setting. Most of the resultant intervals are consonant, implying the tonic chord, while the "A" and "G" notes, appearing with the words "bells are," may imply the dominant seventh chord. Traditional European-based rounds, like "Frère Jacques," usually stay close to the tonic and sometimes dominant harmonies.

"Ah, Poor Bird," figure 4.3, has a different sound; it is more modal than tonal. Notice how the harmonic implications often refer to the relative major (F Major) and the minor dominant (a minor).

FIG. 4.3. "Ah, Poor Bird" Round

Figure 4.4 shows "Ah, Poor Bird" written out as an infinite canon at the octave using the third vocal entrance for the follower voice.

FIG. 4.4. "Ah, Poor Bird" as an Infinite Canon for Two Voices

"Row, Row, Row Your Boat" is another well-known round and harmonically more similar to "Frére Jacques" than "Ah, Poor Bird." It is notated in figure 4.5 as a round for four voices.

FIG. 4.5. "Row, Row, Row Your Boat" Round

Figure 4.6 shows "Row, Row, Row Your Boat" written out as an infinite canon at the octave using the second vocal entrance for the follower voice.

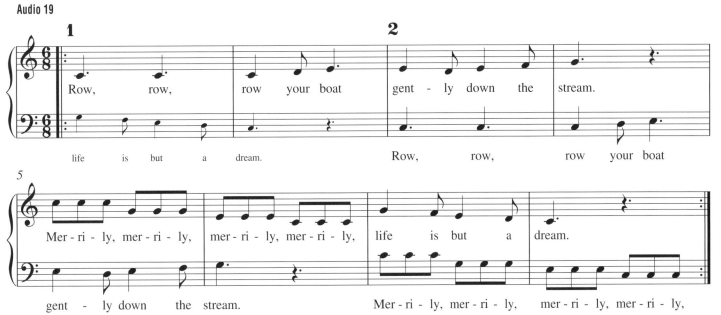

FIG. 4.6. "Row, Row, Row Your Boat" as an Infinite Canon in Two Parts

When we write a canon with a cadential ending it is no longer a round; that is, it is no longer an infinite canon. One could say that it has become a finite canon, as in example 4.7 where "Row, Row, Row Your Boat" comes to a close at the end of the phrase. The canonic treatment in this counterpoint example ends in measure 6 and the phrase closes at measure 8 with a perfect authentic cadence.

Audio 20

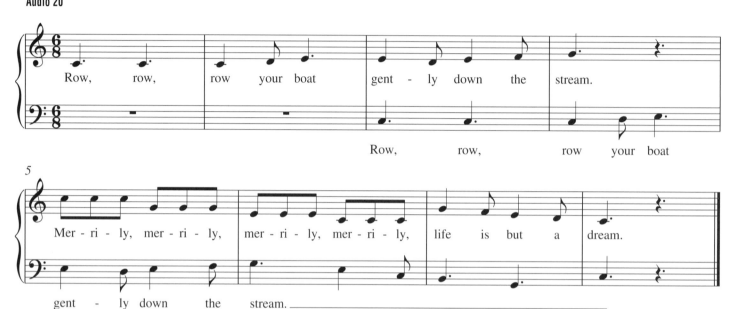

FIG. 4.7. "Row, Row, Row Your Boat" Written as a Two-Part Canonic Phrase

ACTIVITY 4.1. SIMPLE CANON AT THE OCTAVE

Now that you have seen several rounds written out for two voices, realize this traditional Polish melody as a simple two-voice canon at the octave. Using a grand staff with the leader voice in the treble, begin the follower voice as the bass voice at measure 3, and adjust the ending to create one of the cadences learned in chapter 2.

FIG. 4.8. Traditional Polish Melody

ACTIVITY 4.1 VARIATION

For a fun activity, write the melody for Activity 4.1 twice, each time on a separate piece of paper (or in a notation file on two separate staves). Now slide the two pieces of paper back and forth varying the resultant combination of pitches and rhythmic patterns, and notice in how many ways the two voices work together canonically.

"SUMER IS ICUMEN IN"

And now for something Medieval: "Sumer Is Icumen In" may be the most famous canon of all time! It was written sometime around 1260 CE and is one of the first written examples of a canon. It was also sung as a round as long as the mead lasted.

Su - mer is   i - cu - men in ____ Lhu - de sing cuc - cu.   Grow - eth sed and blow - eth med and

springth the w - de nu.   Sing   cuc - cu.   A - we ble - teth   af - ter lomb, louth

af - ter cal - ve cu.   Bul - luc ster - teth, buc - ke ver - teth mu - rie sing cuc - cu.

Cuc - cu,   cuc - cu,   Wel sing - es thu cuc - cu ne swik thu na - ver nu.

FIG. 4.9. The "Sumer" Canon

The two-voice version of the "Sumer" canon in figure 4.10 is a partial transcription from Dufin, "The Sumer Canon: A New Revision" *Speculum*, 63.1 (Jan. 1988). There are many recorded versions of this composition, also sometimes called "The Cuckoo Song."

Audio 21

FIG. 4.10. "Sumer" Partial Transcription as a Two-Voice Canon

BIZET'S CANONIC PASSAGE

Six hundred years later, the famous opera composer Georges Bizet wrote incidental music for Daudet's play *L'Arlésienne* (1872). Although a few musicians appreciated Bizet's music, the play was a big flop. So he extracted four sections of the incidental music and rewrote them for full orchestra. That version of the music was a big success and you may recognize this melody that Bizet treated canonically.

FIG. 4.11. L'Arlésienne Excerpt, Fourth Movement, A Section

L'Arlésienne is the lesser known of Bizet's last two great masterpieces, the other being *Carmen* (1875).

HOW TO WRITE A SIMPLE CANON AT THE OCTAVE

We looked at what defines a canon and two examples that are separated by six hundred years. Now, let's learn how to write one. Canonic technique includes applying our previous work with mixed ratios, non-chord tones, and motivic manipulation.

Step 1: Set It Up. Choose the key, meter, and length of measures. For this example, we will work in F major, 4/4, and eight measures.

Step 2: Outline the Form. The leader voice begins first, the follower voice enters two measures later, and both voices stop at the downbeat of measure 8 where the bass voice moves from scale degrees 5 to 1 and the treble voice steps to the tonic for that traditional perfect authentic cadence sound.

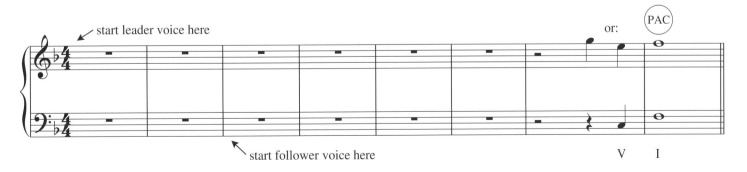

FIG. 4.12. Initial Setup and Outline of the Form

Step 3: Write the beginning of the leader voice. Write a simple diatonic melody for measures 1–2 ("a") that clearly outlines tonic-dominant-tonic harmony. This will let the listener "hear" the key; establishing the key is very important for all tonal music.

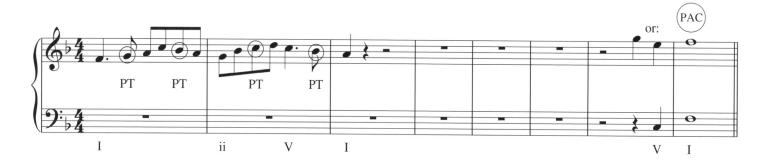

FIG. 4.13. Write the Beginning of the Leader's Voice

For this work, remember to label all non-chord tones and to include Roman numerals under the bass clef (even when only the leader voice is playing). It is important to be aware of the harmonies that you are implying with the melodies you create.

TIPS FOR WRITING CANONS

Tip 1.   An effective rhythmic practice to establish the key is to place the dominant harmony (the V chord) on a strong beat before the follower voice enters, and resolve it to the tonic harmony (the I chord) on the strong beat when the follower voice enters.

Tip 2.   An effective harmonic practice is to create the interval of a third or a sixth between leader and follower when the first note of the follower voice enters (measure 3, beat 1 in this example). You can do this by beginning the melody on the tonic (scale degree) and ending this first part with the mediant scale degree (or vice versa).

Tip. 3.   Moving by step is an effective melodic tool. Leaps are very effective for contrast but only if they do not occur too often.

TIPS FOR WRITING CLASSICAL MELODIES

If you would like that traditional melodic sound, in addition to being mindful of leaps, the following tips will help your melody sound classically historic, as in the late eighteenth and nineteenth century European styles (also called the "common practice period"):

1. Two leaps in a row must outline a triad.

2. If you leap a P5 or more, then immediately change direction.

3. Avoid augmented intervals.

Step 4: Start the Follower. For this exercise, we will keep all notes diatonic to the key. Copy measures 1–2 of the treble voice into measures 3–4 of the bass voice transposed down an octave ("a").

FIG. 4.14. Start the Follower

Step 5: Continue the Leader's Counterpoint Against the Follower. Write good counterpoint in the treble voice measures 3–4 ("b") using mixed ratios to complement the melody in the bass voice. Make sure this new part of the melody supports the implied chords, and label the non-chord tones.

FIG. 4.15. Continue the Leader's Counterpoint

WRITING GOOD COUNTERPOINT

1. If one voice is moving faster, the other voice may move slower and vice versa. This principle, that "each voice takes its turn," allows foreground shifting from one voice to another and helps maintain melodic independence. An exception to this guideline is when both voices are moving in parallel step-wise motion (this works for thirds and sixths in the traditional style).

2. Apply the motivic skills you learned in the previous chapter to your counterpoint. The new counterpoint that you write should often be motivically related to that which came before. Notice how this develops in our example.

Step 6: Continue the Follower Voice at the Octave. Copy measures 3–4 of the treble voice into measures 5–6 of the bass voices, transposed down an octave ("b").

FIG. 4.16. Continue the Follower Voice at the Octave

Step 7: **Continue the Leader Voice.** Write good counterpoint in the treble voice in measures 5–6 ("c") using mixed ratios to complement the melody in the bass voice. Make sure that this new part of the melody supports the implied chords and label non-chord tones, as shown in figure 4.17.

Audio 24

FIG. 4.17. Continue the Leader Voice

Step 8: **Continue the Follower Voice, but Prepare to Cadence.** The next logical step would be to copy measures 5–6 of the treble voice into measures 7–8 of the bass voice transposed down an octave. We would do this if the canonic part of the composition were longer than eight measures. However, we need measure 8 to be the downbeat for the resolution of the perfect authentic cadence, so we must stop the canonic passage before that point. Start copying "c" into the follower voice. At some point, you will leave "c" and make the cadential formula to close the phrase. In this example, we will copy the leader voice's measure 5, beats 1–2 into the follower voice's measure 7, beats 1–2 (down an octave). So "c" begins in the follower voice, then departs from the canonic material and instead prepares for the cadential formula.

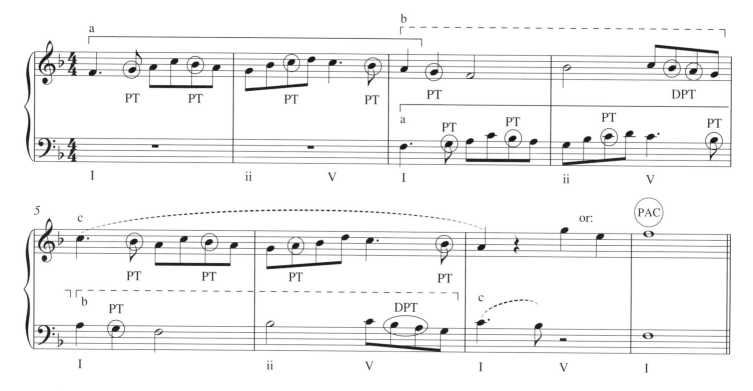

FIG. 4.18. Prepare to Cadence

Step 9: Cadence. Fill in the rest of measure 7 to make the perfect authentic cadence. The canonic passage ends with new counterpoint that realizes a perfect authentic cadence.

FIG. 4.19. Cadence

Step 10: Always double-check your work. Pretend that you are the teacher, and you will see your work in a new light and catch any "oops!" that you may not have seen before. You're done, congratulations!

ACTIVITY 4.2. DISCUSSION OF ROUNDS AND CANONS IN POPULAR MUSIC

Find a simple canon or round in a popular music style that you like and share it with a friend or colleague. Explaining what you have learned to someone else deepens and more permanently settles the knowledge within you.

In contemporary music, canonic imitation is found across a vast musical spectrum of genres including symphonies and heavy metal bands. One well-known example of a canonic passage in popular music is from the Beach Boys' classic "God Only Knows." You can hear it in about the middle of the piece (around 1:16, depending on the recording you select). In making your own selection, the important element is to hear that repetition occur in another voice while the leader voice continues its melody.

Often, canonic imitation like this in popular music is brief, and it may repeat so often that it sounds more like an ostinato passage (see chapter 7).

Here are a few examples:

- Metallica (Hetfield, Ulrich, Hammet), "Welcome Home"
- They Might Be Giants, "Bee of the Bird of the Moth" (end)
- Jethro Tull (Anderson, Abrahams), "Round"
- Queen (May), "The Prophet's Song" (middle)
- Rondellus' "Sabbatum": Black Sabbath's "Verres Militares"
- Cowboy Bebop OST, "Green Bird"
- Rent, "Will I"

ACTIVITY 4.3. WRITING A CANON

Following the steps listed, write a simple canon in the traditional style at the octave, for two voices.

Form:

- Key: Choose F major, G major, D major, or B♭ major
- Meter: 4/4
- Length: 8 measures
- Notes: Use mostly half, quarter, and eighth notes (and rests)
- Interval of the canon: octave

Content:

- The follower voice enters at the downbeat of measure 3.
- The length of canonic treatment should be three to six measures, or more.
- The canon should break before the final cadence (during measure 7).
- The final resolution (PAC) occurs on the downbeat of measure 8.
- Identify all non-chord tones.
- Write Roman numerals under the bass clef.

Here is a map of how the eight measures should be constructed:

Measure	1	2	3	4	5	6	7	8
Leader	a		b		c			
Follower	(rest)		a		b		c' (cadence)	I

FIG. 4.20. Map of Canon

SUMMARY

The canon is one of the most important elements in counterpoint—when the same thing happens at a different point in time in another voice. At any simultaneous point in time the canon, and imitative counterpoint in general, is defined by the contrasts between those voices—different rhythms, moving in different directions, different timbres (instrumental colors). So, there is a temporally, diagonally unifying factor perceived with simultaneous differences. We hear *the same* later on partly because each voice maintains its independence by *being different* at any single point in time. This simultaneous contrast and diagonal sameness is crucial to understanding counterpoint's power and effectiveness. In this chapter we learned about the basic type, or baseline, of canons—the simple canon at the octave (or unison). There are many different types of canonic and imitative writing and we explore them in the chapters to come.

PART II:
IMITATION AND THE CANON

Part I, chapters 1–4, covered music theory fundamentals, and specifically, those related to counterpoint. Part II, chapters 5–7, builds on this foundation by exploring more advanced contrapuntal techniques.

Chapter 5 investigates motivic imitative techniques in two-voice contrapuntal textures. Chapter 6 introduces the ostinato as a non-canonic voice in three-voice textures. And chapter 7 examines canons at intervals other than the octave or unison, the inverted canon, and the double canon.

Imitative Counterpoint

You learned about motivic imitation in chapter 3, and the simple canon (a very specific type of imitation) in chapter 4. Now let's step back for a moment and consider imitation in its broadest sense.

On one end of the imitation spectrum, there is the canon: a very strict set of rules to create a very specific type of imitative relationship between musical lines. What is at the other end of the spectrum? That is, what would be a good example of imitation in its loosest, broadest meaning that is inclusive of all kinds of music? Would it be using ostinato? The ostinato is a repetition of a musical idea, including a bass line or chord changes, and we will study ostinatos in chapter 6. Or, how about the blues? The melody of the first musical phrase (bars 1–4) often repeats in bars 5–8 but with different chords. Or, what about the imitation in so many pop songs where another voice repeats the end of a phrase, overlapping the original voice, but it ends there, almost as a melodic echo, and goes no further? How about the use of digital signal processing in dance music? Often an original line is processed so that it is recognizable but with significant transformation, and this manipulated voice comes in and out, off and on, throughout the piece? Or how about reverberation? The sound is continued, sometimes with a rearticulation of its beginning, although the overall effect is of one sound, not two.

Canon   **Reverberation**

Strict Imitation   **Loose Imitation**

FIG. 5.1. Spectrum of Counterpoint Concepts

Being aware of the broadest applications of imitation opens the widest door for creative possibilities when writing your own music. On another hand, having mastery of in-depth techniques regarding motivic manipulations of multiple lines in a contrapuntal texture opens other creative possibilities that are equally, or possibly even more so but in a different way, meaningful when masterfully applied to create successful compositions.

In this chapter, we will apply the motivic manipulations of the single melodic line to multiple lines, that is, in a contrapuntal context. This is called imitative counterpoint, when motivic imitation is used across multiple voices. We will look at traditional and contemporary examples of imitative counterpoint, starting with the greatest of all contrapuntalists, Johann Sebastian Bach.

J.S. Bach's "Invention No. 3," for two voices, demonstrates a tightly woven fabric of motivic relationships. Please listen to it while following the score. There are many excellent recordings of this piece, including Peter Serkin's *Bach: Inventions; Sinfonia; Duets*; RCA Red Seal (1997).

FIG. 5.2. J.S. Bach, "Invention No. 3"

CANONIC BEGINNINGS AND SEQUENCES

Let's examine some of these motivic relationships. "Invention No. 3" begins with a simple canonic passage at the octave in measures 1–4:

FIG. 5.3. Bach, "Invention No. 3," Measures 1–4

This main melodic idea recurs throughout the composition. Sometimes, it is repeated exactly in its original form; other times, it appears as a real sequence, tonal sequence, or with other motivic manipulations.

Let's look at the intervallic content of the first motive.

FIG. 5.4. Bach, "Invention No. 3," Measure 1

After repeating the motive at the octave in the bass voice in measures 3–4, there is a modified sequence in the treble, beginning on C♯ in the pickup to measure 5, followed by another modification in measure 6.

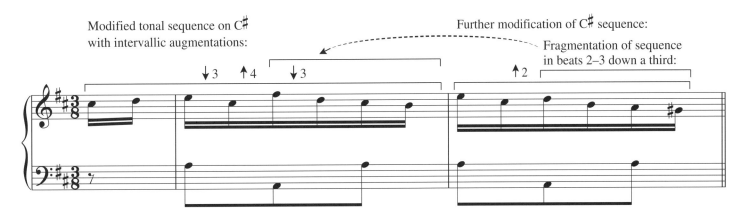

FIG. 5.5. Bach, "Invention No. 3," Measures 5–6

After these interesting motivic manipulations, measures 5–6 are immediately repeated in measures 7–8. Repetition is an effective unifying device, especially when that repetition (measures 7—8) is repeating a modification (measures 5–6) of the original motive (measure 1). That is, it is the same but different: novelty with familiarity. These imitative relationships bring meaning to the music and attract the listener's continued interest.

The first section comes to a close with a modified tonal sequence down a third, minus the pickup notes, in the bass voice (measure 10) followed by a perfect authentic cadence in the dominant key in measures 11–12.

In the following section, the main melodic idea is developed into a four-measure phrase that alternates between voices as a sequence of ascending fifths (what jazz harmony calls an "extended dominant passage"). It begins in the bass voice in measures 12–14 and becomes fully formed with its second appearance in the treble in measures 13–16. The sequence is stated again in the bass voice in measures 15–18, and concludes with an incomplete version in the treble in measures 17–19. Each sequence is up a fifth implying the keys of A major, E minor, and B minor. Notice that these sequences overlap by two measures and how the easing into and out of this passage with incomplete statements of the sequence enhances the fluidity of the composition.

FIG. 5.6. Bach, "Invention No. 3," Measures 11–20. Overlapping sequences of ascending fifths.

ACTIVITY 5.1

Single-measure sequences follow (measures 19–21) and several varied versions of the main melodic idea occur after that. See how many instances of motivic imitation you can find, and then listen to the piece again being mindful of these relationships.

CONTEMPORARY EXAMPLE

This pop tune became a jazz standard and uses two sequences for most of the chorus' melody. Examine the motivic relationships in the first half of the chorus (figure 5.7).

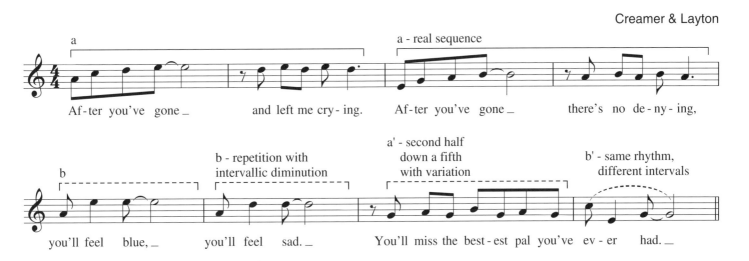

FIG. 5.7. "After You've Gone" Excerpt with Motivic Analysis

Audio 26

See how these motivic relationships are developed further by creating counterpoint with the bass voice (figure 5.8).

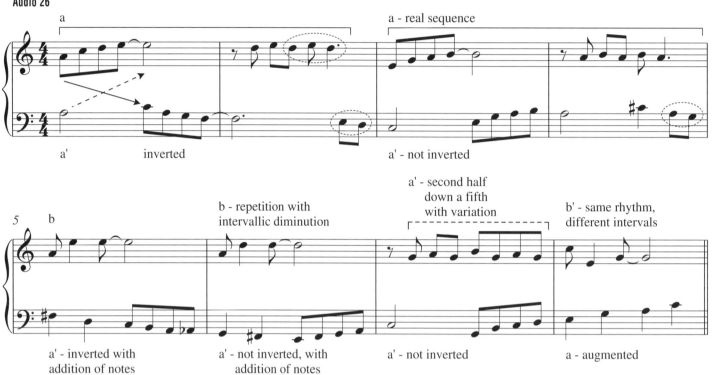

FIG. 5.8. "After You've Gone" Excerpt with Counterpoint

ACTIVITY 5.2

Write a melody in your own style by using sequences and other motivic manipulations. Then add another voice to create counterpoint while continuing to develop those motivic relationships between the voices.

BACH'S MENUET IN C MINOR

Audio 27

For further investigation into the relationships between motives in a contrapuntal texture, let's examine and listen to the first part of "Menuet" from *French Suite No. 2*.

FIG. 5.9. Bach, "Menuet" from *French Suite No. 2*, Measures 1–8

MINUET

The *minuet* (also spelled "menuet") is a moderate dance in triple meter and a common movement in Baroque keyboard suites. These suites emerged from Renaissance music in which instrumentalists played dance pieces defined by tempo, meter, and rhythmic patterns. They often improvised on these movements while entertaining at social gatherings. These dance pieces became concert repertoire in the Baroque period when the multi-movement keyboard suite reached its peak, from 1650–1750.

What makes this passage so effective? Beginning with the harmony we see that the A section modulates from C minor to E♭ major:

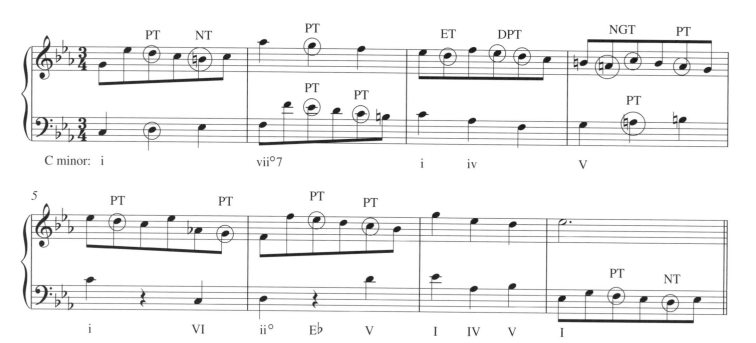

FIG. 5.10. Bach, "Menuet" from *French Suite No. 2*, Harmonic Analysis of Measures 1–8

Melodically, there are two to three ideas primarily defined by their rhythms per measure as in the treble of measure 1 with (a) six eighth notes in a melodic contour, also found, with an inversion of the last note, in measure 6 and in the bass in measure 2; (b) three quarter notes as in the bass of measures 1, 3, 4, (5, 6), and 7, and in the treble in measures 2 and 7; and in (c) six eighth notes similar to "a" but with a contrasting melodic contour in measures 3, 4, 5, and in the bass in measure 8.

ACTIVITY 5.3

Answer the following questions about this passage:

1. What is the motivic relationship between the treble voice in measure 1 and the bass voice in measure 2?

FIG. 5.11. Treble Measure 1, Bass Measure 2

    a. There is no relationship.

    b. The ascending sixth is augmented to an octave and the last step is inverted.

    c. The whole motive is inverted.

2. What is the motivic relationship between the bass voice in measure 1 and the treble voice in measure 2?

FIG. 5.12. Bass Voice Measure 1, Treble Voice Measure 2

    a. Sequence

    b. Inversion

    c. Sequence and inversion

3. What is the motivic relationship between the bass in measure 1 and the bass in measure 3?

FIG. 5.13. Bass Voice Measure 1, Measure 3

    a. Sequence and inversion

    b. Sequence and intervallic augmentation

    c. Inversion and intervallic augmentation

4. What is the motivic relationship between the bass in measure 1 and the bass in measure 4?

FIG. 5.14. Bass Voice Measure 1, Measure 4

    a. Inversion

    b. Sequence

    c. Retrograde

Here is the passage with motivic analysis:

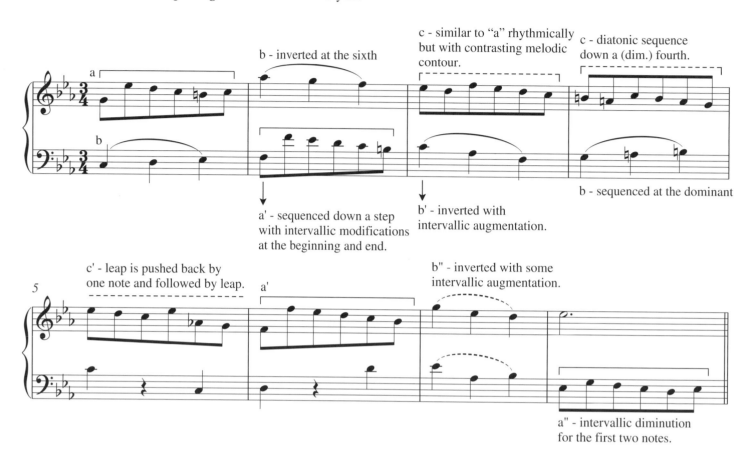

FIG. 5.15. Bach, "Menuet" from *French Suite No. 2*, Motivic Analysis of Measures 1–8

Now let's put it all together:

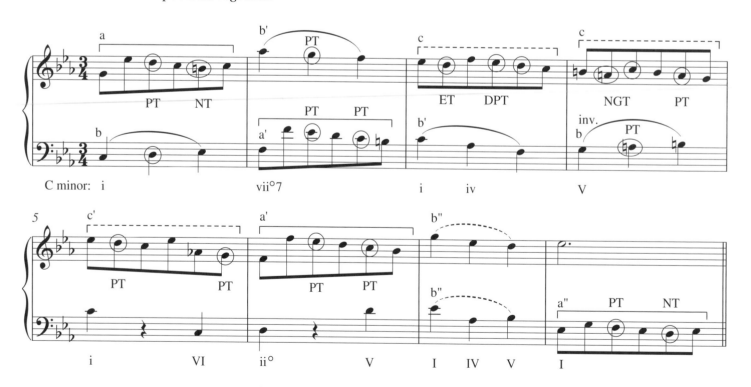

FIG. 5.16. Bach, "Menuet" from *French Suite No. 2*, Combined Harmonic and Motivic Analysis of Measures 1–8

Imitative counterpoint offers many motivic relationships between notes as seen in the preceding examples. In the composing process, what comes next should always be considered in conjunction with what came before. Meaning in music is communicated through the relationships that we create, whether that be through the use of pitches (with some rhythmic consideration) as discussed here or in any other combination of musical elements including rhythm, timbre (instrumental colors), articulation, texture, and density.

DOUBLE COUNTERPOINT

Double counterpoint, also called "invertible counterpoint," immediately exchanges the music of each of the voices, in their appropriate registers, after the initial statement. And that's it! Here's an example of the double counterpoint technique applied to the jazz standard "Hindustan."

Hindustan

Audio 28

Oliver Wallace, Harold Weeks

FIG. 5.17. "Hindustan," Measures 1–16 with Double Counterpoint (a/b: measures 1–8, b/a: measures 9–16)

In traditional practice, the double counterpoint technique maintains a pleasing, consonant sound by restricting chord tones to the harmonic intervals of unison, third, sixth, and octave; non-chord tones, used appropriately, are also allowed. We will explore this technique in its traditional manner while understanding that we can apply it to our own music, as seen above with "Hindustan," without the historical restrictions regarding consonances and dissonances.

Step 1. Write original material for two voices. For this example we begin with two measures of two-voice counterpoint with clear harmonic implications using only the thirds, sixths, and octave harmonic intervals. Even though the fifth is a consonant interval, its inversion, the fourth, was considered a dissonant interval in the traditional practice. For this reason the fifth is avoided, unless it is treated as if it were a non-chord tone, in double counterpoint.

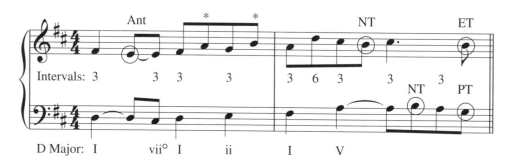

* The fifth is handled as if it were an appoggiatura for this technique.

FIG. 5.18. Initial Statement in Preparation for Double Counterpoint

Step 2. Immediately repeat the music with the voices exchanged.

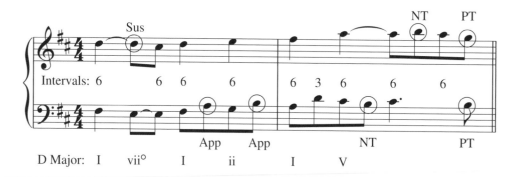

FIG. 5.19. Double Counterpoint

Audio 29

Step 3. Complete the phrase. Combine the two four-measure passages, and add a cadence to conclude the phrase:

FIG. 5.20. Double or Invertible Counterpoint: a/b followed by b/a

Restricting harmonic intervals to thirds, sixths, and octaves (unisons) maintains that historically consonant sound. And yet, as mentioned before, double counterpoint can be applied to any style of music. Here is a contemporary example using a pentatonic scale where all of the intervals are considered consonant.

Audio 30

FIG. 5.21. Double Counterpoint with the C Major Pentatonic Scale

Double Counterpoint in "Invention No. 6"

Bach's "Invention No. 6" begins with a tour de force of double counterpoint that also includes a very high level of syncopation.

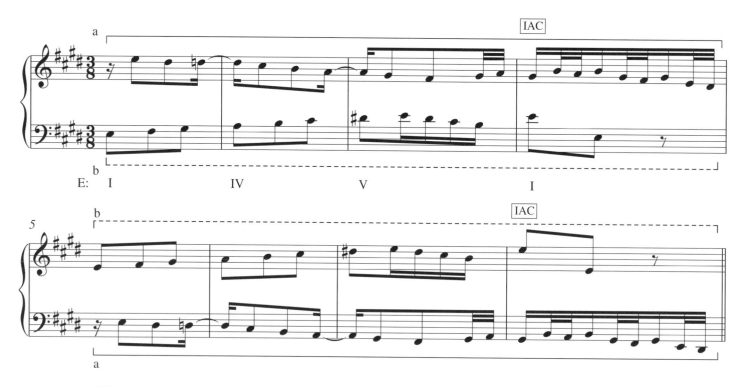

FIG. 5.22. Bach, "Invention No. 6," Measures 1–8

Now, listen to all of "Invention No. 6," and see how many times you hear these four measures of music in their original and double counterpoint versions. Double counterpoint is another way to maximize one's musical resources.

ACTIVITY 5.4. FREE-STYLE CONTEMPORARY COMPOSITION

In this activity, you will create a free-style contemporary composition for two voices using imitative counterpoint.

Select a favorite melody for your cantus firmus. It can be in whatever style you prefer (jazz, pop, Latin, rock, metal, folk, etc.). Create a grand staff for sixteen measures, and intersperse the motives from this melody throughout the sixteen measures, possibly alternating placement from the treble staff to bass staff from time to time. Now, fill in the empty spaces with motivic manipulations from the melodic segments you have already set. Remember to be aware of your harmonic implications and to make the melodic gestures meaningful; the music should flow in an effective manner. Then, write a short narrative describing the music, specific motivic relationships, and your creative decisions. Writing a narrative about one's musical decisions is often insightful in ways not previously considered.

SUMMARY

This chapter focused on passages from several contemporary compositions as well as three compositions by J.S. Bach with detailed motivic, harmonic, and melodic analysis. We investigated how these components work together to create effective imitative counterpoint including double counterpoint. We used contemporary and traditional examples in the application of these techniques, and you created your own composition using these techniques in a contemporary style.

Activity 5.3. Answers

1. b, 2. c., 3. c, 4. b

CHAPTER 6

Ostinatos and Accompanied Canons

Ostinatos may be considered another type of imitation. However, an ostinato does not change. Its powerful unifying impact comes from being repeated. Most often that repetition is immediate and continual in the same voice although, in a broader sense, an ostinato can be shared between multiple voices. When a bass line ostinato is repeated, it is traditionally called a ground bass or basso ostinato. When the ostinato is a chord progression, it is traditionally called a chaconne and often contains a ground bass, too. Both the ground bass and chaconne are usually short passages of music that are repeated throughout a tune. Many elements of music can be structured to function as an ostinato; for example, a repeating rhythmic pattern as in a drum set pattern or a recurring timbral envelope as in post-spectral music.

On the large, architectural scale, an ostinato occurs, in a more broader sense, whenever the song itself is used for improvisation. That is, as the harmonic progression is repeated over and over again for the soloist's improvisations, the song form itself has become an ostinato. And by far the most common ostinato use in popular music is the bass ostinato, traditionally called the ground bass.

A DAY IN TAHITI

This contemporary example uses a ground bass. It sequences the first measure down a step, with some intervallic diminution, in the second measure to create a two-measure ostinato that repeats throughout the A section.

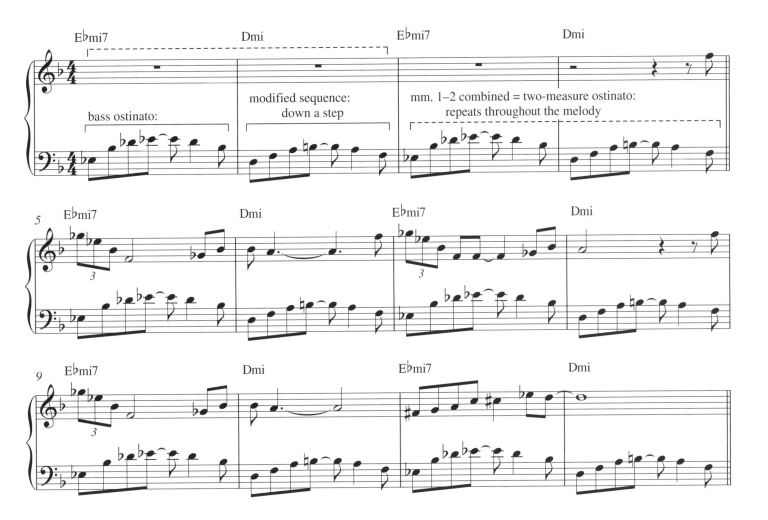

FIG. 6.1. "A Day in Tahiti" Excerpt, Example of Bass Ostinato

Notice also the almost ostinato-like melody. The first two-measure section in the treble voice then recurs twice, the first time with some slight variation and the second time as an exact repetition.

MOVING FORWARD WITH THE GROUND
(Or "Under the Ground" as in Purcell's "Lament")

"When I Am Laid in Earth," from Henry Purcell's opera *Dido and Aeneus* (premiered 1689), is a song that uses a ground bass. The bass ostinato is six measures long, begins by chromatically descending to the dominant, and concludes with a traditional cadential formula (scale degrees 4-5-1). This ostinato is repeated eleven times. The song, or aria, is also called "Dido's Lament" because Queen Dido sings this lament before stabbing herself to death as her lover, Aeneas, sails away.

FIG. 6.2. Purcell, "When I Am Laid in Earth" from *Dido and Aeneus*, Bass Ostinato

What chords support this chromatically descending ground bass? Add the first vocal phrase, and we can see the harmonic implications. (Non-chord tones are circled.)

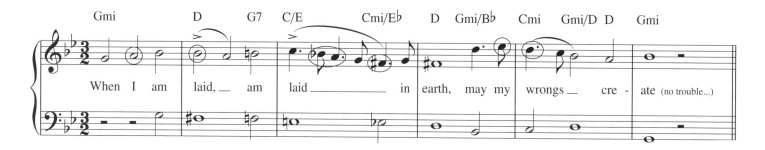

FIG. 6.3. Purcell, "Dido's Lament," Bass Line and Vocals, Measures 1–6

The sadness of the music supports the poignancy of the lyrics:

When I am laid, am laid in earth, may my wrongs create
No trouble, no trouble in thy breast;
Remember me, remember me, but ah! forget my fate.
Remember me, but ah! forget my fate.

RECITATIVE AND ARIA

In opera, two basic types of singing are used. The *recitative* is used to describe the action or plot and is delivered fairly quickly with a simple rhythm, one note per syllable, and as a single line (monophonic). The other type of singing is the *aria*, like "Dido's Lament." It is lyrical, full of musical expression for the voice with many melismas (multiple notes per syllable of text). The recitative precedes the aria and sets the stage for the emotional outpouring and/or reflection of sentiment in the aria.

ACTIVITY 6.1. WRITE YOUR OWN MELODY TO PURCELL'S GROUND BASS

Using Purcell's ground bass, create your own melody in your own musical style. Include harmonic analysis (chord symbols over the treble clef or Roman numerals under the bass clef), and be mindful of your use of non-chord tones.

OSTINATO WITH CANON

Figure 6.4 shows the beginning of "Dido's Lament" with a version of the melody arranged canonically at the octave; leader and follower voices are separated by two measures.

FIG. 6.4. Purcell, "Dido's Lament," Bass Line with Canonic Treble Lines (modified melody), Measures 1–6

OSTINATO FOR MULTIPLE VOICES

What if the bass ostinato is made up of two parts instead of one? Both parts must work together as a short unit that repeats. For example, figure 6.5 presents a three-measure bass ostinato:

FIG. 6.5. Bass Ostinato 1

Let's add another voice on top of that first one:

FIG. 6.6. Bass Ostinato 2

Do you see the motivic relationship between the two voices when we combine them together (figure 6.7)? They are playing the same music an octave apart and separated by three beats. This is also an example of double counterpoint: a/b followed by b/a.

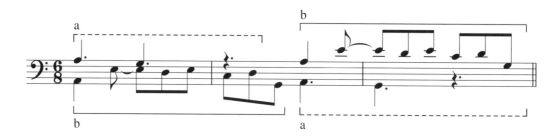

FIG. 6.7. Bass Ostinati 1 and 2

Now let's add the melody:

FIG. 6.8. Bass Ostinati 1 and 2 with the Melody

Audio 31

And finally, add one more contrapuntal technique to this atmospheric example to complete the composition. We can make the melody canonic by adding a follower voice an octave down in measures 5–9:

FIG. 6.9. "Ancient Winds" Bass Ostinati 1 and 2 with Melody in Canon

When there is a canon with an additional, non-canonic line, it is called an accompanied canon. Look carefully at the bass ostinati. Notice that the two voices exchange places every three beats. In this case the canon is accompanied by two bass ostinati working together in double counterpoint.

The "Sumer" canon is another example of a canonic piece with two voices providing the bass ostinato in double, also called "invertible," counterpoint.

RETURNING TO "SUMER"

In chapter 4, we learned that "Sumer" is a round and a canon. Here are the first twelve measures of "Sumer," written out as a four-voice canon.

FIG. 6.10. "Sumer Is Icumen In," Four Canonic Voices, Measures 1–12

The original manuscript indicates that it is to be sung as a four-voice canon with two additional voices for a total of six voices. What are the remaining two voices doing? They are creating a special bass ostinato. At first glance the ostinato appears to be four measures long, it repeats throughout the piece:

FIG. 6.11. "Sumer Is Icumen In" Bass Ostinato 1

But there are two bass voices. Here are the first four measures of the other bass voice.

FIG. 6.12. "Sumer Is Icumen In" Bass Ostinato 2

Do you see the motivic relationship between these two examples?

Measures 3–4 of the second voice are measures 1–2 of the first voice. Have we seen this motivic manipulation before? Yes! Take a look at the two voices together.

FIG. 6.13. "Sumer Is Icumen In" Two-Voice Bass Ostinato

Play this on a keyboard and listen: measures 1–2 and 3-4 sound exactly the same because the music of the first and second voices exchange places. This is another example of double, or invertible, counterpoint: "a" over "b" immediately followed by "b" over "a."

FIG. 6.14. "Sumer Is Icumen In" Two-Voice Bass Ostinato in Double Counterpoint

An additional, interesting piece of information: "Sumer" was written in the Medieval 2 period (1000–1400 CE) when accompanied canons with the non-canonic line(s) in the bass were refered to as "pes," Latin for "foot." In other words, the canonic lines are standing on the foot, the "pes." In the "Sumer" case, the pes is an ostinato of two voices in double counterpoint.

ACTIVITY 6.2.
CONTEMPORARY EXAMPLES OF OSTINATOS

What is more common in so many styles of popular music than the ostinato? It is not the ostinato itself that makes the music so effective; rather, it is how the composers/performers write and improvise over the repeating material. Here are a few examples: why do these work so well? How do you use ostinati in your music?

- Avicii, "Wake Me Up"
- Alesso, "Cool"
- Beatles (McCartney), "What You're Doing"
- Beyonce (Tegor and Bogart), "Halo"
- Cream (Bruce), "Sunshine of Your Love"
- Daft Punk (Williams and Rodgers), "Get Lucky"
- Herb Ellis (Giuffre), "A Simple Tune"
- Mancini, "Peter Gunn Theme"
- Pink Floyd (Waters), "Money"
- Radiohead (Yorke), "Creep"
- Shaw, "Partita for 8 Voices"
- Yellow Jackets (Ferrante, Haslip, Lawson, Russo), "Wildlife"

When a non-canonic line accompanies a canon, the piece is called an *accompanied canon*. Both the "Ancient Winds" and "Sumer" canons are accompanied canons. The additional, non-canonic voice is *accompanying* the canonic voices. This non-canonic voice is often a bass ostinato, repeating a short section of material, as often found in contemporary music.

PACHELBEL'S CANON IN D

Possibly the most popular canon from the classical (Baroque) tradition is *Canon in D* by Johann Pachelbel. One finds many interesting settings of this piece including comedic string performances, folk rants, and Korean hip-hop versions.

"Canon in D" begins with the non-canonic line in the bass called the "ground bass" or a "basso ostinato."

FIG. 6.15. Pachelbel's "Canon in D" Bass Ostinato (or Ground)

This bass ostinato repeats throughout the composition, every two measures.

The leader voice, Violin 1, enters with "a" at measure 3 after the first statement of the basso ostinato:

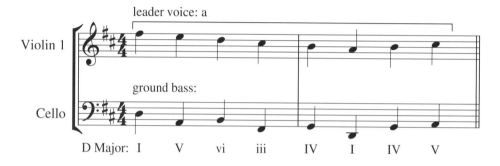

FIG. 6.16. "Canon in D" Measures 3–4

When Violin 2, the first follower voice, enters two measures later (canon at unison), the leader voice makes good counterpoint ("b") to support "a" by harmonizing the "a" material down a third up until the last note when it provides the sixth, the inversion of the third:

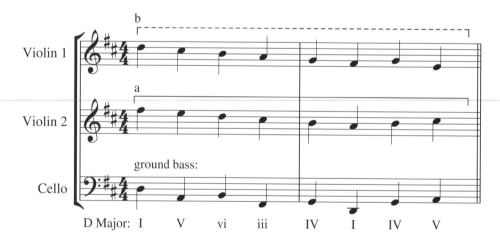

FIG. 6.17. "Canon in D" Measures 5–6

Then, after another two measures, Violin 3 enters making this a three-voice canon with accompanying basso ostinato for a total of four voices. Violin 2 now carries the good counterpoint of "b" that the leader voice had in measures 5–6, and Violin 1 makes new counterpoint "c" to work harmoniously with the three other voices.

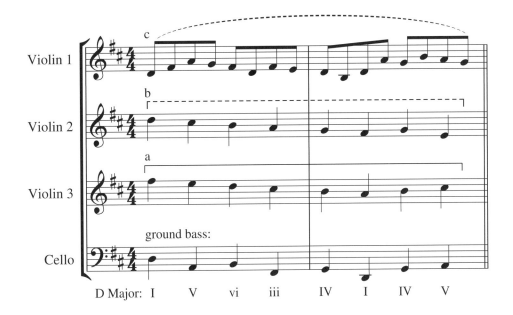

FIG. 6.18. "Canon in D" Measures 7–8

The canonic technique continues in the upper three voices throughout the piece. Here are the first eight measures as described above.

FIG. 6.19. "Canon in D" Measures 1–8

CONTINUO

As you listen to recordings of this piece, you may hear a keyboard part that is not written out in the score. This is called a "continuo" in which the bass line is played, not only by the cello (or other bass instrument), but also by the keyboardist who adds chords, too. The harmony was indicated by "figured bass," a shorthand code of numbers similar in function to the chord symbols in a lead sheet (see figure 2.18).

RUNNING A DIVISION

Notice that the Violin 1 begins playing eighth notes at measure 7. These faster moving notes increase line independence, because they break the unison rhythmic pattern between the voices. The music sounds like it is moving faster, even though the beat remains constant, as the notes continue to rhythmically subdivide, adding sixteenth and thirty-second notes to the texture. *These variations are motivically related and create imitative counterpoint within the canonic technique that continues throughout the piece.*

Sometimes, the added notes sound like ornamentations of the melody, as if someone is improvising each time around the "head," as jazz musicians call a melody, or, in this case, the two-measure ostinato. There is a long history (thirteenth through eighteenth centuries) around this practice. It is referred to as extemporized "divisions" over a ground, "running a division," and "breaking a ground."

As mentioned in earlier chapters, the written art of counterpoint emerged from the improvisatory practices of musicians through the ages. These musicians' gigs, just like today, were often at social events where people would dance, and some speculate that the number of notes/beats in the ground (for "Canon in D" this is eight) may be related to the repetition of the dance steps. As in: dance in one direction for a certain number of steps, and then turn for the next repetition of the dance pattern when you hear the ground repeat.

ACTIVITY 6.3.

Write your own counterpoint with quarter, eighth, and sixteenth notes as a way of "running a division" over this ground by completing measures 3–4 in the treble voice.

FIG. 6.20. Activity 6.3

ACTIVITY 6.4. POPULAR PACHELBEL SETTINGS

The ground bass and chord progression of Pachelbel's "Canon in D" has remained a recognizable feature in music, crossing cultures, centuries, and musical styles. The piece is often played at weddings, and has been used for many movies and television commercials. Beyond this, numerous popular songs are based in part or wholly on "Canon in D."

Here are a few examples. Select one of these or find another popular setting that you like and describe it in a brief narrative. Work to describe the piece in musical terms. For example, "the melody is repeated in the saxophone and the guitar switches to distorted sustained tones that rise and fall in contrary motion with the melody," rather than "the beautiful melody and ambient atmospheric distortion reminded me of the ocean just before a thunderstorm." Consider the musical elements and how they interact: melody, harmony, timbre, texture, rhythm, tempo, style.

- Aphrodite's Child, "Rain and Tears"
- Blues Traveler, "Hook"
- Brian Eno, "Three Variations, Part 3"
- Coolio, "I'll C U When U Get There"
- Delerium, "Paris"
- Green Day, "Basket Case"
- Jacques Loussier Trio, "Canon in D Major"
- My Chemical Romance, "Welcome to the Black Parade"
- Pet Shop Boys, "Go West"
- Piano Guys, "Rockelbel's Canon"
- Sanguine Predicament, "Canon in D"
- Tupac, "Life Goes On"
- Vitamin C, "Graduation Friends Forever"

ACTIVITY 6.5. WRITING AN ACCOMPANIED CANON USING GROUND BASS

Create your own three-voice composition with two voices in imitative counterpoint over a ground bass using either Pachelbel's "Canon in D," Purcell's "When I Am Laid in Earth," or "Sumer Is Icumen In" (choose one). There will be two upper parts in imitation (that may or may not be canonic) with a third voice in the bass, the bass ostinato.

CONCLUSION

Ostinatos are prevalent in contemporary music throughout the world and across the ages in traditional styles. In this chapter we examined the influence and presence of ostinato in both old and new repertoire and considered its relevance in our own work as composers, arrangers, singer/songwriters, and improvisers. We saw the application of ostinato in two of the most famous classical pieces of all time: the "Sumer" canon and Pachelbel's "Canon in D." You reviewed the use of these techniques in many popular songs and wrote your own. Ostinato, with and without canon, is one of the most frequently used and extremely effective contrapuntal devices that can improve the effectivenes of your own creative efforts. Do not hesitate to apply this technique to your own compositions. As seen here, it works across many styles and genres.

CHAPTER 7

More Canonic Techniques

In this chapter, we will learn three new canonic techniques. The first is how to write a canon at an interval other than the octave, the second is how to write an inverted canon, and third, how to write a double canon.

1. Canons at intervals other than the octave are identified in the same way that we identified the canon at the octave: the interval identifying the canon is the distance between the first note of the leader voice and the first note of the follower voice.

2. In canon by inversion, the follower voice of a canon is inverted, moving note to note by the same interval as the leader voice but in the opposite direction. This is also called a canon in contrary motion, or canone in moto contrario.

We will look at some contemporary examples and "Variation No. 12" from the *Goldberg Variations* of Johann Sebastian Bach, which uses both of these techniques.

3. Double canon: When two canons are happening at the same time. Often, the two canons are motivically related, as we will see in an example by Brahms.

When you are comfortable with these procedures, you will find them frequently useful. You are strongly encouraged to write by hand each example as you read through the text, which may significantly speed up your mastering of these powerful techniques.

CANONS AT INTERVALS OTHER THAN THE OCTAVE

A canon at another interval occurs when the follower voice is transposed so that it is a sequence of the leader voice rather than at the same pitch as the leader voice. As mentioned above, these canons are named by the interval formed between the first note of the leader voice and the first note of the follower voice.

Let's write a canon at the sixth. Creating any canon at an interval other than the octave begins the same as a canon at the octave. That is, we will write the beginning of a melody for the leader voice.

Step 1: Write the "a" for the leader voice. Here is a two-measure example for "a."

G: I

FIG. 7.1. Leader Voice Begins, Measures 1–2

Step 2: Transpose "a" diatonically up a sixth. Transposing diatonically means that we are staying in the same key, which sometimes means that a M6 becomes a m6 or a M2 becomes a m2, etc., but the interval number stays the same.

FIG. 7.2. Follower Voice Enters at the Sixth, Measures 3–4

Audio 32

Step 3: Prepare the two entrances.

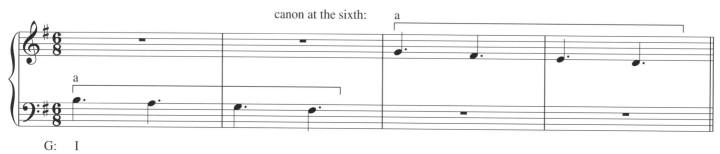

FIG. 7.3. Leader and Follower Entrances for a Canon at the Sixth

Note: The first note of the bass voice and the first note of the treble voice make the interval of a sixth. Do not invert the notes (the note of higher pitch always stays on top). It does not matter whether it is a M6 or a m6 because this is a diatonic transposition.

Audio 33

Step 4: Write good counterpoint for "b" in the leader voice to support the harmonic implications of "a" in the follower voice (measures 3–4). Then transpose "b" up a sixth for the follower voice in measure 5–6.

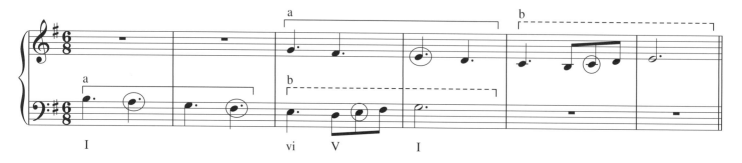

FIG. 7.4. Leader Voice Counterpoint against "a" in Follower

Note: The second note in this canonic line—leader voice "A," follower voice "F♯"—has changed its function from being a non-chord tone to becoming a chord tone because of the reharmonization. (Likewise, the third note that was a chord tone is now a non-chord tone.) It is important to be aware of the harmonic implications of the counterpoint and how melody notes may change function more often when creating a canon at an interval other than the octave (or unison).

Step 5: Continue adding to the voices. Write good counterpoint, "c," under "b," that supports those harmonic implications and continue in this manner. Continue transposing up a sixth for the follower voice each time, until closing with a final cadence. In this example, the cadence occurs immediately after "c" in the leader voice and with modification for the cadence at the end of "b" in the follower voice.

Audio 34

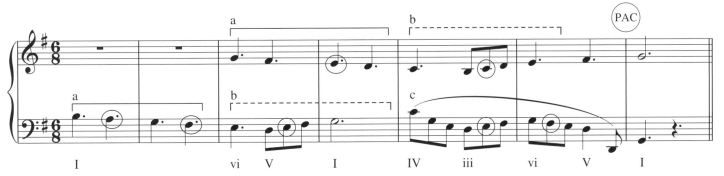

FIG. 7.5. Canon at the Sixth

ACTIVITY 7.1.

Write a six- to eight-measure two-voice canon at an interval other than an octave or unison and end with a perfect authentic cadence.

Here is a contemporary example in a medium Latin style:

Audio 35

FIG. 7.6. Contemporary Example of Canon at the Ninth

CANON BY INVERSION

Canon by inversion (or *canone in moto contrario*) occurs when the follower voice moves from note to note the same intervallic distances as found in the leader voice, *but each interval is moving in the opposite direction.*

This is an example of the beginning of an inverted canon at the unison.

Audio 36

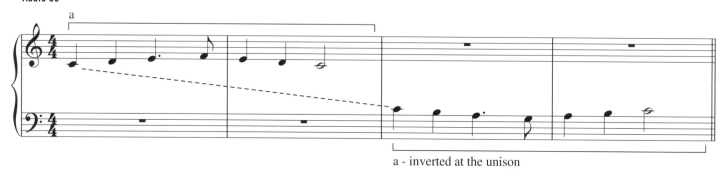

a - inverted at the unison

FIG. 7.7. Inverted Canon at the Unison (Beginning)

Canons can be inverted at any interval. In this next section, we will study the canon by inversion at the fourth.

COMPOSING A CANON BY INVERSION

Step 1: Create the beginning of a melody. This melody starts on the tonic and ends on the dominant.

FIG. 7.8. Create Melody

Step 2: Because this will be a canon by inversion *at the fourth,* **first transpose the original canonic line down a fourth.** (It could be down or up by a fourth; this example places the follower voice beneath the leader voice.)

FIG. 7.9. "a" Transposed Down a Fourth

Audio 37

Step 3: Now invert the transposed canon. Match the intervallic distance of each interval diatonically in the transposed version, but move in the opposite direction.

FIG. 7.10. Motive "a" Transposed and Inverted

Notice how the original melody moves down in a series of steps to end at the dominant. When inverted at the fourth, the effect is quite excellent, as it moves up by steps to the tonic. If the original melody ended on the subdominant and was inverted at the fifth, it would also end on the tonic!

Audio 38

Step 4: Set the leader and follower entrances together for the beginning of the canon.

FIG. 7.11. Canon by Inversion at the Fourth (Beginning)

Step 5: Now write "b"—good counterpoint in the treble voice, measures 3–4, to support the harmonic implications of "a," inverted at the fourth, in the bass voice.

While there are multiple possibilities, here is one answer that can be "b":

FIG. 7.12. "b"

Audio 39

Adding "b" to the canon:

FIG. 7.13. Canon by Inversion at the Fourth, Measures 1–5

MAKING THE CONNECTION

When writing a simple canon at the octave, or any interval, we simply copied "b" and placed it at the diatonic transposition of that interval in the other voice. This does not work for an inverted canon because each new interval in the follower voice must move in the opposite direction of the leader voice's interval. Only the first note of each voice will define the interval of the canon (in this case, at the fourth). If the fourth occurs between the corresponding notes of the leader and follower voices at any time in the future, it is purely coincidence.

Therefore, we must continue connecting to each subsequent note by the same intervallic distance found in the corresponding leader voice's interval *but in the opposite direction.*

Step 6: Use the same interval between "a" and "b" from measure 2 to 3 in the leader voice, but apply it in the opposite direction to find the correct next note in the follower voice moving from measure 4 to 5.

ACTIVITY 7.2.

Which of the following "b" segments for the follower voice is correct?

FIG. 7.14. Follower Voice "b" Options

Audio 40

Here are measures 1–7 with the correct answer:

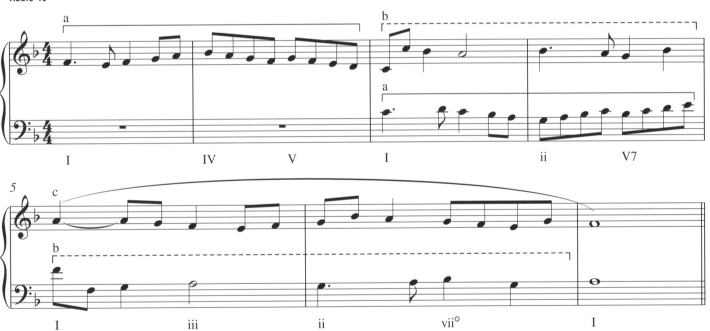

FIG. 7.15. Inverted Canon at the Fourth, Measures 1–7

Note: The interval connecting "a" to "b" in the leader voice is a M2 *down* (D to C, measures 2–3). So the interval connecting "a" to "b" in the follower voice is a m2 *up* (E to F, measures 4–5). Remember, we are staying diatonic, in the key, so it does not matter whether the interval of the second is a M2 or a m2; just use the notes in the scale.

ACTIVITY 7.3. WRITE YOUR OWN PHRASE USING CANON AT ANOTHER INTERVAL BY INVERSION

Write your own four- to eight-measure phrase using the canon by inversion technique. Here is a contemporary example of an inverted canon at the fourth.

Audio 41

Tangerine Mood

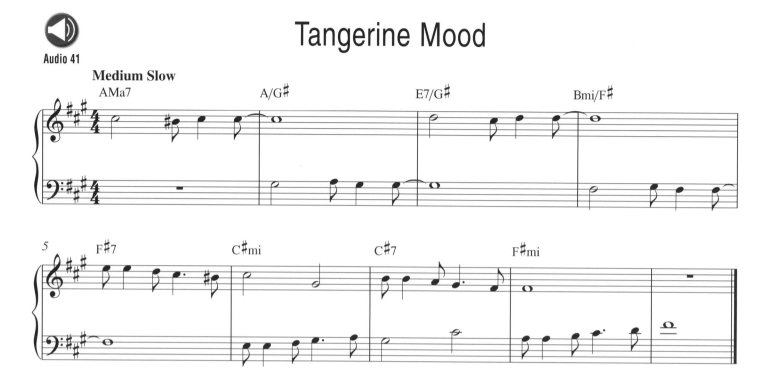

FIG. 7.16. "Tangerine Mood," Contemporary Example of an Inverted Canon at the Fourth

BACH'S "GOLDBERG VARIATION NO. 12"

Goldberg Variations, for harpsichord, begins with an aria and continues with thirty variations. The full score is available at the International Music Score Library Project, and there are many excellent recordings. Every third variation is an accompanied canon in ascending intervallic order: at the unison, at the second, at the third, etc. "Variation No. 12" is an inverted canon at the fourth with a third, non-canonic bass line.

Figure 7.17 indicates the individual lines and harmonic implications of measures 1–4 for "Variation No. 12."

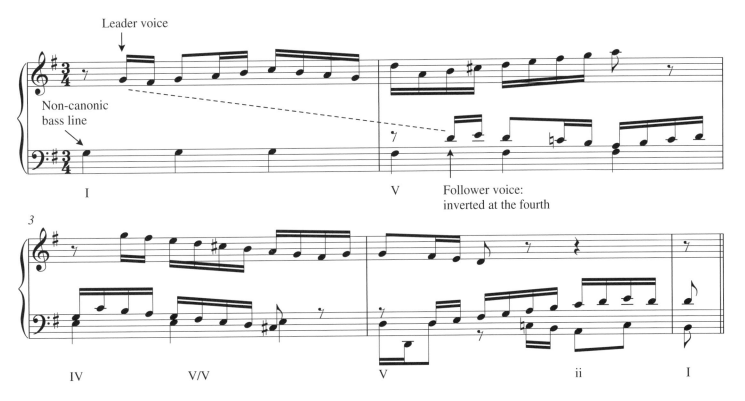

FIG. 7.17. "Goldberg Variation No. 12" Measures 1–4

Notational Note: When two voices share the same staff, the notes' stem directions indicate the different voices. The inverted line begins in measure 2 in the tenor voice.

Identifying the Contrapuntal Techniques in *G.V. #12*

- The soprano and tenor lines are canonic. The bass line is non-canonic. This is an accompanied canon.

- The interval between the first note of the soprano (leader) voice and the first note of the tenor (follower) voice is the interval of a fourth. This is an inverted canon at the fourth.

- The follower voice is not a simple transposition of the leader voice; each interval is going in the opposite direction because this is a canon by inversion.

- Putting it all together: This is an example of an accompanied inverted canon at the fourth.

How does Bach make these multiple contrapuntal techniques work so well together? Here is "a" in the soprano voice, measure 1.

FIG. 7.18. "Goldberg Variation No. 12," Leader Voice, Measure 1

Notice that the non-canonic line clarifies the harmonic implications. This is a benefit to consider when you are wondering whether you want to write an accompanied or unaccompanied canon. In this case, the bass voice is repeating the tonic note, and we clearly hear G major, the tonic chord.

This is a canon at the fourth, so the first note of the follower voice, in the tenor, begins a fourth below the first note of the leader:

FIG. 7.19. "Goldberg Variation No. 12," Follower Voice, Measure 2 (Inverted at the Fourth)

In figure 7.20, each interval in the tenor line of measure 2 is moving the same distance (diatonically) but in the opposite direction to the corresponding intervals in the soprano line found in measure 1.

Here is "a" in the soprano, leader voice followed by an inverted "a" at the fourth in the tenor, follower voice with the accompanying non-canonic bass line.

FIG. 7.20. "Goldberg Variation No. 12," Measures 1–2, "a" with Bass Line

Now, for "b," Bach writes good counterpoint to support the tenor voice and harmonic implications of measure 2.

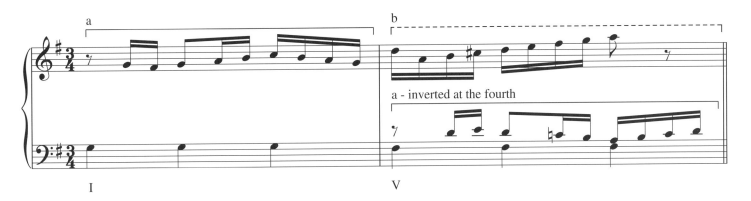

FIG. 7.21. "Goldberg Variation No. 12," Measures 1–2, "a" and Leader Voice's "b" with Bass Line

Motive "a" was moved down by a fourth into the follower voice. Will he do the same thing for "b"? No, but why not?

Because this is a canon by *inversion.*

The simple transposition down a fourth, the way the first note of "a" began in the follower voice, will not carry forward for a canon by inversion. All new notes must match their corresponding interval in the leader voice but by moving in the opposite direction.

Look at how "b" begins with an ascending fifth from the last note of "a": G up to D. That movement of the fifth must be maintained, *and* it must move in the opposition direction (by inversion).

So, because D is the last note of the follower voice's "a," what will the first note of the follower voice's "b" be? That is G, down a fifth.

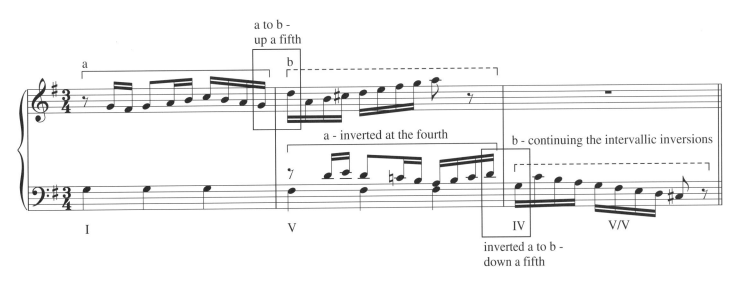

FIG. 7.22. "Goldberg Variation No. 12," "a" and "b" in the Leader and (inverted at the fourth) Follower Voices

Now you know the procedure to create the inverted canon.

Notice that "c" begins down a step from the last note of "b" in the leader voice. If there are rests, simply move forward over the rests until you reach the next note to determine the interval.

FIG. 7.23. "Goldberg Variation No. 12," "a," "b," and "c" in the Leader and (inverted at the fourth) Follower Voices

Note: Remember that the inverted voice's connecting melodic interval (a to b, b to c, etc.) matches the melodic distance of the interval in the leader voice but moves in the opposite direction. The *resulting harmonic intervals between voices will not be the same in the inverted passage* as it was in the original passage (unless this happens by coincidence).

Now let's add the canonic voices to the non-canonic bass line. Listen again to measures 1–4, and consider the new motivic shapes that emerge from the manipulations created by an inverted canon at the fourth.

FIG. 7.24. "Goldberg Variation No. 12," Measures 1–4. Showing continuation of the canon by inversion technique for generating "b" and "c" in the follower voice with the non-canonic bass line.

ACTIVITY 7.4. CREATING A CANON BY INVERSION AT AN INTERVAL OTHER THAN THE OCTAVE OR UNISON

Following the steps outlined above, write a short inverted canon for two voices, with or without (your choice of) a third, non-canonic bass line. Write two four- to six-measure phrases. Use chord symbols above the treble line and remember to clearly articulate the phrases.

DOUBLE CANON OR LOVE AND BEAUTY

Thirteen Canons for Women's Voices, No. 4, Op. 113, "No. 6," by Johannes Brahms (1833–1897)

We have studied and written counterpoint for mostly two voices, sometimes three. However, as seen in the accompanied canons, contrapuntal music can be written for three voices or four, as in the Pachelbel canon, and six as in the "Sumer" canon. The famous contrapuntal composer of the sixteenth century, Palestrina, often wrote canons for eight or more voices!

The next composition that we will look at, Brahms' "Canon No. 6," is written for four voices, and all of them are canonic.

FIG. 7.25. Johannes Brahms and his *Thirteen Canons for Women's Voices*

The score is available at the International Music Score Library Project and there is a recording by the Chamber Choir of Europe, Brilliant Classics Records, BC94262.

This canonic choral setting of a short love poem roughly translates:

As long as beauty will persist
With eyes on earth to gaze
You will not escape love.

The composition begins with each voice entering independently, and then the repeated section sets the loop boundaries for all four voices. After this, there is a final ending, and although not so noted by the composer, the repeated section could be performed many times as a round, an infinite canon.

Soprano 1 enters first, the leader voice.

FIG. 7.26. Brahms, "Canon No. 6." Soprano 1 entrance, pickup to measure 1.

Soprano 2 enters next with the pickup to measure 5.

FIG. 7.27. Brahms, "Canon No. 6." Soprano 2 entrance, pickup to measure 5.

What is the canonic relationship between Soprano 1 and 2? It is a canon at the unison, separated by four measures.

Alto 1 begins its own line between the soprano entrances with the pickup to measure 3:

FIG. 7.28. Brahms, "Canon No. 6." Alto 1 entrance at pickup to measure 3.

And Alto 2 enters with the pickup to measure 7, at canonic unison with Alto 1.

Look at the soprano and alto lines; are there any noticeable motivic relationships?

FIG. 7.29. Brahms, "Canon No. 6." Soprano and alto entrances in comparison.

They are in melodic inversion to one another with the alto beginning a third below the soprano. The motivic relationship of the two voices is an inverted canon at the third.

Canonic Techniques in "Canon No. 6"

All four voices are in canonic relationship with one another. Soprano 1 and soprano 2 are in simple canon at the unison. Alto 1 and alto 2 are in their own simple canon at the unison. This is an example of a *double canon* because there are two separate canons occurring simultaneously.

In addition, due to the particular motivic relationship between the soprano and alto lines, this is also a double canon inverted at the third.

So lange Schoenheit wird bestehn
from Dreisehn Kanons, Op. 113

Johannes Brahms

FIG. 7.30. Brahms, "Canon No. 6" from *Thirteen Canons*, Op. 113

The repeated section contains all of the contrapuntal content with the first full measure of half notes ornamented to chromatically moving quarter notes. Soprano 1 starts with the beginning of its line, soprano 2 on its measure 5, alto 1 at measure 3, and alto 2 at measure 7 (see fig. 7.30). If the canon were written as a round, it would look like this:

* Parts 2 and 4 are inverted and
transposed down a diatonic third.

FIG. 7.31. Brahms' "Canon No. 6" as a Round

How does Brahms make this work harmonically? Let's combine the four parts onto one staff and look at all the notes. If we look at the round's repetition, there are only four measures of music. Here is the piano reduction with chord symbols:

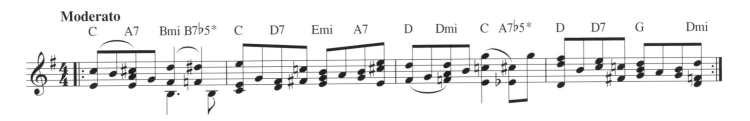

FIG. 7.32. Piano Reduction with Chord Symbols.* The augmented sixths may be seen as chromatic passing tones.

Through stepwise, often chromatic motion, and some strong voice leading, Brahms creates a rich and sonorous four-voice double canon.

ACTIVITY 7.5. APPLYING THESE TECHNIQUES

Create a single or double canon at an interval other than the octave or unison. Write for two to four voices for sixteen to twenty-four measures. You may incorporate canon by inversion (optional) and it can be in any musical style.

SUMMARY

These advanced canonic techniques—canons at other intervals, canon by inversion, and double canons—are relevant and applicable in many progressive applications. Look for opportunities to expand your original ideas and bring meaning and unity to your compositions with these effective techniques.

PART III: ADVANCED TECHNIQUES AND APPLICATIONS

Chapter 8 digs deeper into the puzzles and riddles of canonic technique by exploring retrograde and the enigmatic crab canon. Chapter 9 explores canons by rhythmic augmentation and diminution including the mensuration canon where multiple rates of motion happen at the same time. Chapter 10 demonstrates the application and combination of contrapuntal techniques in contemporary music using examples created by Berklee Online Counterpoint students.

CHAPTER 8

Alchemy and Counterpoint

In this chapter, we will look at motivic manipulations for two-voice counterpoint that further develop the techniques studied in chapters 4, 6, and 7. We will examine both historic and contemporary examples that demonstrate new ways to manipulate motives and phrases in two-voice textures upside down, inside out, and backwards. The crab canon is a tour de force of these new techniques, and we will review compositions with this technique including an example from Bach's magnum opus *The Musical Offering*.

MAGICIAN, MUSICIAN, AND SCIENTIST

The ongoing search for that single source from which everything diverse arises recurs and transforms across artistic mediums and scientific inquiries. New methodologies and innovative techniques come and go but the search continues.

Counterpoint grew out of the European Renaissance as part of the alchemical search. The right contrapuntal design may lead to divine perfection just as mercury may transform base metals into gold. The proto-scientific and artistic/creative methods were viewed as partners, parallels in this quest for the divine.

THEILE, *MUSICALISCHES KUNSTBUCH*, SELECTIONS FROM NUMBER 7

The following example of two-voice counterpoint is from an important seventeenth-century publication, *Musicalisches Kunstbuch* (written sometime between 1670–1680). Johann Theile (1646–1724), an ardent proponent of the alchemy/counterpoint connection, composed these pieces, and we will look at example number 7 to see how the motivic usages—that is, the imitative contrapuntal manipulations—relate to the original counterpoint as David Yearsley noted in his publications[1] with the modern notation in figure 8.2.

---

[1] Yearsley, David. "Alchemy and Counterpoint in an Age of Reason." *Journal of American Musicological Society*, vol. 51, no. 2 (Summer, 1998), p. 233. And Yearsley, David. *Bach and the Meanings of Counterpoint*. Cambridge University Press, Cambridge, 2002. p. 81.

Audio 42

FIG. 8.1. Original Version, Theile, "Example Number 7"

Let's start by examining the intervals between the two voices.

FIG. 8.2. Theile Example with Intervallic Analysis

…and the harmonic implications:

FIG. 8.3. Theile Example with Harmonic Implication Analysis

Theile applies many different imitative techniques to this original five-measure phrase. We will look at seven of them, and you will recognize the manipulations from your motivic and contrapuntal work in chapters 4 and 6.

Technique 1. Double or Invertible Counterpoint. Double counterpoint occurs when the two voices are exchanged: the bass becomes the treble, and the treble becomes the bass. Theile maintains that traditional, consonant sound in this example because the harmonic intervals are restricted to octaves, sixths, thirds, and unisons.

Audio 43

FIG. 8.4. Double (or Invertible) Counterpoint

Audio 44

Technique 2. Each Voice in Melodic Inversion. Melodic inversion moves from note to note in the opposite direction.

FIG. 8.5. Melodic Inversion for Each Voice

Audio 45

Technique 3. Melodic Inversion in Double Counterpoint. Now switch the melodically inverted lines: treble into the bass voice and the bass into the treble voice (with appropriate octave adjustments) and the melodically inverted lines are now in double counterpoint.

FIG. 8.6. Melodically Inverted Lines with Double Counterpoint

Audio 46

Technique 4. Retrograde. Return to the original line of counterpoint and state each voice in reverse: starting with the last note and ending with the first note.

FIG. 8.7. Retrograde on the Original

Audio 47

Technique 5. Retrograde in Double Counterpoint. The retrograded lines can now switch voices to create their own double counterpoint.

FIG. 8.8. Double Counterpoint with Retrograde

Audio 48

Technique 6. Retrograde Inversion. Go back to the inverted lines and state them from last note to first note, in reverse order, for the retrograde inversion version. [Or go back to the retrograded lines and move each note by the same intervallic distance but in the opposite direction.]

FIG. 8.9. Retrograde Inversion (retrograde with melodic inversion for each line)

Audio 49

Technique 7. Retrograde Inversion in Double Counterpoint. Switch the treble and bass voices of the retrograde inversion version for retrograde inversion in double counterpoint.

FIG. 8.10. Retrograde Inversion with Double Counterpoint

CONTEMPORARY EXAMPLE

We looked at a new age-type melody, *Ancient Winds*, in chapter 6, as an example of canonic voices over two ostinatos in double counterpoint. Here is another version of that melody with counterpoint derived from the ostinatos and the melody. Notice how this melody works with several of the permutations described above.

FIG. 8.11. "Ancient Winds" with Multiple Permutations

ACTIVITY 8.1.

Write a four- to six-measure two-voice phrase, and permutate it in three of the seven permutations presented. Notice how these different manipulations create effective transformations.

CRAB OR RETROGRADE CANON

The crab canon takes the double counterpoint and retrograde permutations and brings them together in a unique way. There are neither leaders nor followers in a crab canon. Both voices start together and end together. Both voices sing the same line of music, only one is singing it backwards. In addition, halfway through they exchange voices and sing the first half of each others' parts in retrograde for the second half of the piece.

There are two preferred ways to make a crab canon. To start from the beginning with both voices and move forward to the end is not one of them. You can:

1. Start from the middle with both voices and work your way out to the ends; or

2. Start from the ends with both voices and work your way towards the middle.

We will create a crab canon with a contemporary sound.

WRITING A CRAB CANON

Let's start from both ends and work our way towards the middle using a simple swingy, folk-like sounding melody. Adjust octaves as necessary.

Step 1: Write measure 1 in both voices.

Audio 50

FIG. 8.12. Crab Canon, Measure 1

Step 2: Place the retrograde of the treble voice, measure 1, in the last measure of the bass voice (one octave down).

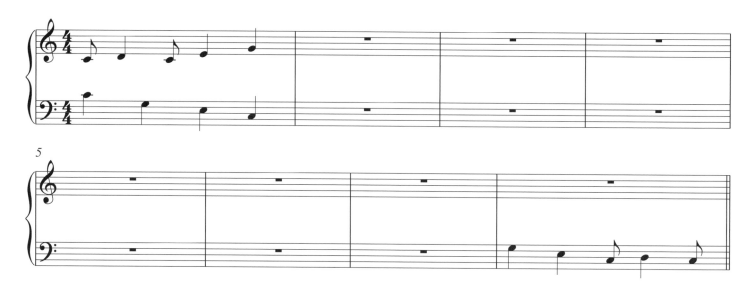

FIG. 8.13. Measure 1 with the Bass for Measure 8

Audio 51

Do the same with the bass voice, measure 1: retrograde it in the treble for measure 8 (one octave up).

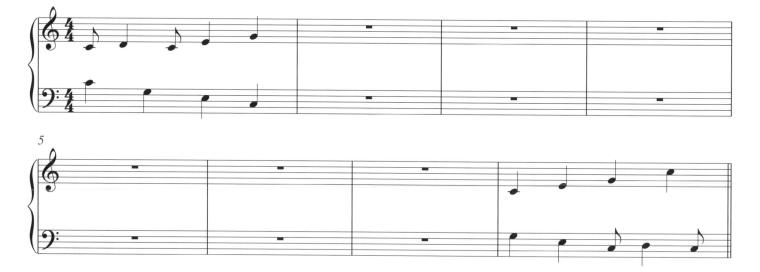

FIG. 8.14. Crab Retrograde of Measure 1 in Measure 8

Audio 52

Step 3: Now write measure 2, or you might try writing two measures at a time for measures 2–3.

FIG. 8.15. Adding Measures 2–3

Step 4: Put the treble voice, measures 2–3, retrograded in the bass voice's measures 6–7.

FIG. 8.16. Treble Measures 2–3 Retrograded in Bass Measures 6–7

Step 5: And do the same with the bass, measures 2–3: put it in the treble, retrograded, at measures 6–7.

FIG. 8.17. Measures 1–3 Retrograded in Measures 6–8

Now bring it all together with the middle two measures, measure 5 in double counterpoint being the retrograde of measure 4. Notice that symmetrical rhythmic patterns work well when retrograded. This also applies to harmonic implications. Pre-plan what chords may be implied in your notes when they are retrograded for ease in the harmonic progression.

Step 6: Create measure 4 and retrograde it while switching the voices for measure 5.

FIG. 8.18. Crab Canon Completed

Step 7: This was a simple example with triadic melodic and harmonic figures. An important element in writing a successful crab canon is the willingness to go back and "do over." If a motive that sounds good in its original version doesn't work, for whatever reason, in its retrograded form, then go back and rework the original version until it is satisfactory both coming (original) and going (retrograde). A crab canon is a great way to practice the *back and forth* of compositional editing that is intrinsic to an excellent outcome in any style of music using any type of craft.

BACH'S *MUSICAL OFFERING*, "CANON 1 A 2 CANCRIZANS"

The famous crab canon from J.S. Bach's *Musical Offering* (1747), is identified in the score as "Canon 1 a 2 Cancrizans." You may recognize the opening motive as one of the examples from chapter 4.

MUSICAL OFFERING

The *Musical Offering* is a collection of canons, a few fugues, and other pieces all based on a theme given to Bach by Frederick II of Prussia, to whom he dedicated the work. It was composed late in Bach's life and represents some of the finest canonic work of all times.

If the *Strange Paths* website is available, you may want to view their Möbius strip that illustrates through animation how the crab canons work using this one by Bach as an example.

http://strangepaths.com/canon-1-a-2/2009/01/18/en/

Here is Bach's canon in modern notation.

FIG. 8.19. Bach's Crab Canon in Modern Notation (*MO*, CC1a2)

The full score is available at the International Music Score Library Project, and there are many excellent recordings. Notice that the "crabbing" (double counterpoint with retrograde) begins in measure 10. You can trace the crab-like motion by following note to note in the opposite direction with the two voices exchanged, and you can also trace the notes by starting at the end, going backwards, and comparing this to the notes beginning at measure 1 and going forward, also with the other voice.

There are many chromatic notes in this canon. Here is an analysis of the harmonic implications that these two lines suggest, measures 1–8.

FIG. 8.20. Bach's Crab Canon, Harmonic Analysis, Measures 1–8

ACTIVITY 8.2. WRITING A CRAB CANON

You can choose either of the procedures described in this chapter to write your own eight-measure crab canon (only one was presented in detail). You can write it in a modal, tonal, chromatic, traditional, or contemporary style; it is your choice. Remember to go back and forth as you work. If the original melodic segment you are retrograding just doesn't work, do not be shy to go back and adjust the original line. When both lines come together, they may lose direction or forward motion; don't hesitate to adjust and try again. The "back and forth" part of the composing process is very important when working with the crab canon.

Note: Asymmetrical rhythms often sound awkward in retrograde. When a syncopated pattern is off the beat in the original line, it is often on the beat in retrograde. Symmetrical divisions of the bar or beat often work well.

SUMMARY

In this chapter, you learned about contrapuntal permutations for two-voice counterpoint by studying contemporary and historic musical examples. You then applied the double counterpoint and retrograde manipulations to understand the crab canon by following a contemporary piece as it is assembled; analyzing "Canon 1 a 2 Cancrizans" from the *Musical Offering*; and by writing your own original crab canon.

PUZZLE AND RIDDLE CANONS

Gioseffo Zarlino, the famous Renaissance music theorist, claimed that the canon represents the highest level of composition. If you would like to look more deeply into these types of canons, see "puzzle" and "riddle" canons.

CHAPTER 9

Canons of Rhythm

Canon, as mentioned before, means "rule," and we have examined several different types of canons, or rules, that create various types of compositions with specific contrapuntal relationships. The simple canon emerged from long-standing folk traditions of round singing at the unison or octave. A canon at another interval, other than the octave or unison, adds another layer, or rule, to the procedure. The canon-by-inversion rule makes the follower voice move in the opposite direction, and the crab canon flips the voices and starts moving backwards (retrograde) halfway through the composition. All of those procedures manipulated pitch relationships.

This chapter focuses on *rhythmic* rules for melodic lines whose rhythms are proportionally related to each other. These rules, called prolation or mensuration, were popular from the thirteenth to seventeenth centuries and then had a resurgence of popularity in the twentieth century. Proportional rhythmic procedures of augmentation and diminution are also used today in minimalist styles and in film scoring, too.

Canons by proportional rhythmic augmentation or diminution use the same melody line in two or more voices, but each voice moves forward at its own pace. The relationship of pace between voices is proportional. For example, the leader voice is playing the melody with its original note durations and the follower voice is playing it twice as fast, or three times as fast. In canons by rhythmic augmentation or diminution, both voices start and end at the same time. Historically, this type of rhythmic permutation is called *prolation*, and canons made with this procedure are called *mensuration canons*. In this chapter, we will describe, examine, and construct mensuration canons historically and in modern styles.

CANON BY (RHYTHMIC) AUGMENTATION

Audio 55

Let's begin with a simple melodic phrase:

FIG. 9.1. Melody for Canon by Augmentation

In a canon by augmentation, one voice is moving slower than the other voice, and this is usually in a simple proportional relationship. Let's try moving twice as slow.

FIG. 9.2. Melody moving twice as slow.

Audio 56

Here are both the original and slower moving voices together.

FIG. 9.3. Canon by Augmentation: Both Voices Together

When one voice is moving twice as slow as the other, it takes twice as long to complete the same melodic line as seen above.

NOTATION AND RHYTHM

At this point, a brief summary of some metric considerations will be helpful, as you prepare to select a time signature for your canon by rhythmic augmentation or diminution. Writing mensuration canons includes fitting multiple lines of different rhythms into a composition that uses one time signature. Indicating multiple time signatures at the same time may also be an option. The composer may select either solution. The following summary of meters as used in classical music can help the composer choose the correct time signature(s).

The time signature 6/8 is called a *compound* meter because the beat subdivides into three parts. In *simple* meters like 4/4 or 2/4, the beat *subdivides* into two parts. Both 2/4 and 6/8 have two beats per measures. *Compound time* counts the dotted notes as the beats, not their subdivisions, unless the music is moving at a really, really slow tempo. Compare these measure subdivisions in simple and compound meters:

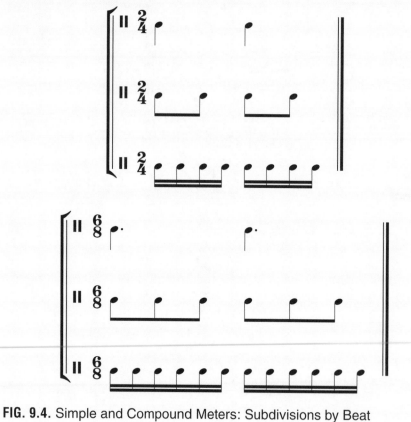

FIG. 9.4. Simple and Compound Meters: Subdivisions by Beat

When triple divisions occur within simple meter or when duple divisions occur within compound meter, the unusual subdivision of notes are indicated by placing a number within a bracket or accompanying the beaming over or under the notes. This notation also accommodates quintuplets and other subdivisions of the beat as well.

The following Avalou (Yanvalou) example is in 6/8 time. This is an example of compound *duple* time—that is, two beats per measure, with each beat subdividing into three parts. The woodblocks have four equally spaced articulations across the measure in contrast to the two beats per measure with subdivisions of three equal articulations each (as expected in 6/8 compound time) in the bass, conga, guiro, and cowbell. Those last three instruments, in combination, also subdivide the beat into six equal articulations. This creates a rhythmic texture of 2:3:4:6.

Audio 57

Maracas Bay Avalou

Ronald Aqui and Rellon Brown

FIG. 9.5. "Maracas Bay Avalou." Score excerpt and audio courtesy of Ronald Aqui and Rellon Brown. Note: There is some variation between the notation and this performance.

CANON BY DIMINUTION

Canon by diminution occurs when the rhythmically permutated line is moving faster. This often occurs in simple proportional relationships to the original line.

Audio 58

Figure 9.6 is a melody in 6/8 time.

FIG. 9.6. Melody in Compound Time

Audio 59

In figure 9.7, the bass line moves faster, in a 3:1 proportional relationship with the original line.

FIG. 9.7. Permutated Melody Moves Two-Thirds Faster than the Original Line

The rhythmically permutated line finishes in one-third of the time it takes the original line to finish. It is moving forward at a rate that is two-thirds faster than the slower moving line.

In this next example, the faster moving line is in a 2:3 proportional relationship with the original line:

Audio 60

FIG. 9.8. Permutated Melody Moves One-Third Faster than the Original Line

The rhythmically permutated line in figure 9.8 finishes in two-thirds of the time it takes the original line to finish. It is moving forward at a rate that is one-third faster than the slower moving line.

CLARITY OF METER

Notice the faster moving line in measures 1 and 3 of figure 9.8. There are three equal articulations of quarter notes in both measures. (The middle quarter note is written as two tied eighth notes to indicate, with the second eighth note, that the music is moving into the next beat.) What time signature does that sound like? Here is how that would look in 3/4 time. Notice how much easier it is to read the faster moving line.

FIG. 9.9. Canon by Diminution in Simple Time

Rhythmic permutations of melodic lines create changes in beat patterns. Often, duple and triple subdivisions of the measure are happening at the same time. In these cases, the composer/arranger has two choices:

1. Select one baseline meter and adjust the other voice to fit by using syncopations and ties, or

2. Use two separate time signatures to optimize rhythmic clarity.

Audio 61

Here is how that would look for our canon by diminution:

FIG. 9.10. Canon by Diminution Using Multiple Time Signatures

ACTIVITY 9.1.

Select one of the above melodies, or create your own, and write a canon by augmentation or diminution. Complete the quicker-moving line with additional counterpoint of your own choosing so that it continues until the end of the slower moving line.

PROLATION AND MENSURATION

Prolation, also called "mensuration," techniques are similar to canons by diminution. They refer to proportional rhythmic relationships between voices using the same melodic line. Compositions created with this canonic technique (rule) were popular in the late medieval era, specifically in the motets and cyclic masses of the fourteenth century Ars Nova period. Prolation and mensuration continued through the Renaissance and into the Baroque period and even into the modern period, as found in the works of twentieth century composer Conlon Nancarrow and the minimalist composers.

The word "prolation" is from medieval Latin "prolatio," meaning "bearing" or "manner." If the manner of the division was by thirds, then the prolation was called a *major prolation*; if reduced by half or quarters it was called a *minor prolation*.

Major Prolation

To perform a *major prolation* is to create a faster moving line by reducing that line in thirds—for example, changing dotted half notes into quarter notes (3:1). In modern notation, that is three quarter notes occurring in the prolated line during the duration of one dotted half note in the original line:

FIG. 9.11. Major Prolation, Diminution by Two-Thirds

If the dotted half notes were changed to half notes (3:2), then the durations of the notes would be reduced by one third.

FIG. 9.12. Major Prolation, Diminution by One Third

CREATING A MENSURATION CANON

Now that you know the major and minor prolations, we are ready to create a mensuration canon. Let's use the "Row Your Boat" melody from chapter 4.

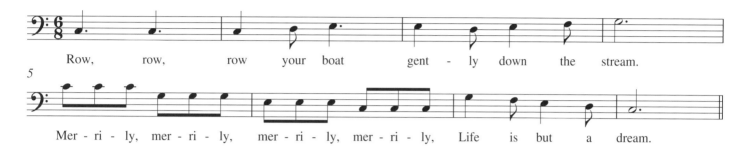

FIG. 9.13. "Row, Row, Row Your Boat" Original Melody

Apply a minor prolation. That is, reduce each note value by half:

FIG. 9.14. First Minor Prolation ("Row, Row, Row Your Boat")

Instead of eight measures to complete the melody, it is finished in four measures. Here are the two lines together:

FIG. 9.15. Original Line with First Minor Prolation ("Row, Row, Row Your Boat")

There are several solutions to complete the prolated line. You could write free, imitative counterpoint, or copy (again) the prolated version, or you could write something combining parts of both of these options. Consider the original line and whether or not the prolated version will work well over the second half of the original melody. What do you think? Listen for the melody at the original speed in the bass and then twice as fast, and repeated, in the treble. Can you hear it?

Audio 62

FIG. 9.16. First Minor Prolation Repeated to Complete the Second Phrase ("Row, Row, Row Your Boat")

Let's add a third line by performing another minor prolation on the prolated line:

FIG. 9.17. Original Line Moving Four Times Faster ("Row, Row, Row Your Boat")

Putting all three lines together, with the prolated lines repeating, creates our version of a three-voice mensuration canon. Other options for completing the prolated lines would be to create free imitative counterpoint that works well with the slowest moving line or combining some free counterpoint with parts of the prolations or even prolating some of the newly created free counterpoint. In the following example, the faster moving lines are the minor prolations (created above) of the original line and separated by register and timbre to assist in listening. Can you hear all three versions of the melody at the same time? Focus on one line, then another, and then "step back" aurally and hear them all at the same time.

Audio 63

FIG. 9.18. Three-Voice Mensuration Canon ("Row, Row, Row Your Boat")

ACTIVITY 9.2.

Write your own two-voice mensuration canon using only an eight-measure single melody line. Apply minor or major prolation to the faster moving line, and repeat that line's prolation to complete the eight measures.

JOSQUIN DES PRÈZ'S MENSURATION CANON

Now, we will examine Josquin des Prèz's "Agnus Dei II 'Ex una voces tres,'" from his *Missa L'Homme armé super voces musicales* (1502). This piece is a *riddle canon*. The original manuscript shows only one line of music, but there are three time signatures. (A copy of the manuscript can be seen in the Wikipedia article for this Mass.) The cryptic notation indicates that three voices sing the melody, each voice at its own rate. The slowest moving voice is the tenor (common time) and the two faster, prolated, voices move forward with the bass voice at cut time and the treble voice at cut time in triplets.

Audio 64

The tenor voice begins on A:

FIG. 9.19. "Agnus Dei II," Tenor Line in Modern Notation

The bass line begins on D and moves twice as fast. It is in minor prolation to the tenor:

FIG. 9.20. "Agnus Dei II," Bass Line

And the treble voice moves three times as fast, in major prolation above the tenor:

FIG. 9.21. "Agnus Dei II," Treble Line as Triplets

The treble line might look better in a different time signature:

FIG. 9.22. "Agnus Dei II," Treble Line with Triple Meter

Like the "Row, Row, Row Your Boat" example, all voices in a mensuration canon begin at the same time.

Here are the three voices of "Agnus Dei II" combined, using multiple time signatures.

FIG. 9.23. "Agnus Dei II"

Listen to this piece; one recommended recording is by the Tallis Scholars (Gimell Records, 1989). Do you hear the melody moving forward at three different rates of speed at the same time? Excellent! Another recommended recording is by the group Alarm Will Sound (Nonesuch Records, 2009) with a modern twist including improvisation.

In figure 9.23, notice the new music of the faster moving lines in the latter part of this piece. Their prolations finish halfway through for the bass and one-third of the way through for the treble. The endings of the prolations for these voices are indicated in the following example. The treble voice completes the melody with the downbeat of measure 9 and the bass voice is finished by measure 13's downbeat.

treble line
completes
the melody here:

bass line completes
the melody here:

FIG. 9.24. "Agnus Dei II." Prolation endings marked in the treble and bass voices.

Notice the imitative relationships between the bass and treble voices. Look carefully at the score; you may want to refer to the single line notations of each voice in the following two examples. See if you can uncover another secret to this riddle canon.

Bass line measures 13–25:

FIG. 9.25. "Agnus Dei II" Bass Line, Measures 13–25

Treble line measures 9–25:

FIG. 9.26. "Agnus Dei II" Treble Line, Measures 9–25

The secret is that the 3:2 prolation is now applied to the new music of the treble and bass voices after they complete the original melody. The treble prolates the bass line's notes from measures 13–25 into its measures 9–17, beat 1. Remember that each voice maintains its own time signature: treble in 3/4 (moving faster: 3) and bass in 2/4 (moving slower: 2). Compare figure 9.25 with the first line of figure 9.26.

In the concluding section, the treble at measure 17 moves back to G and then measures 18–20 are repeated in 21–23 with just a slight variance in the rhythms of the repeated G's in measure 18. Measure 24 continues the alternation of D with G and ends on F for the final cadence in measure 25.

Critically listen to "Agnus Dei II" again while following the score (modern notation) and consider the prolated lines including the *prolation within the prolation* of the bass and treble voices after they finish their prolations of the tenor voice.

More on Proportional Rhythmic Relationships

Proportional rhythmic relationships are powerful generating devices. Even non-pitched instruments can be prolated to make a mensuration canon.

Here is a sixteen-measure line for the bass drum:

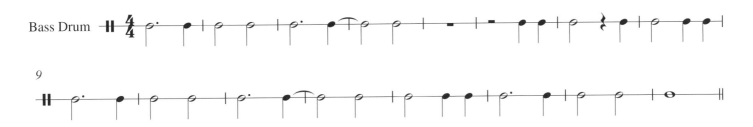

FIG. 9.27. Bass Drum Line

With a minor prolation, it becomes an eight-measure line for the washboard.

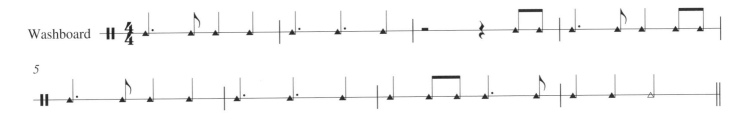

FIG. 9.28. Bass Line with Minor Prolation for Washboard

With another minor prolation on the washboard's minor prolation, it becomes a four-measure line for the snare drum.

FIG. 9.29. Washboard Line with Another Minor Prolation for the Snare Drum

Now, let's put all three lines together for a percussion trio using proportional relationships to create a mensuration canon.

FIG. 9.30. Percussion Trio. Original line with two minor prolations.

The next step is to complete the faster moving lines for the subsequent measures after the prolations. This can be done with free (imitative) counterpoint and/or more prolations. The imitative counterpoint employed here is retrograde. Yes, some of the motivic manipulation techniques learned in previous chapters can also be used on non-pitched percussion instruments.

Snare line with retrograde:

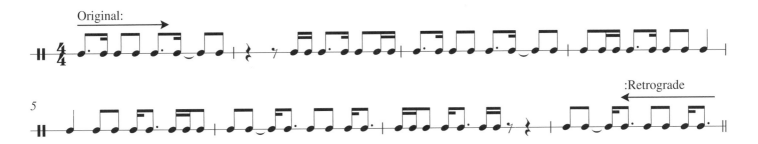

FIG. 9.31. Snare Line. Measures 5–9 are in retrograde to measures 1–4.

The "prolation times two" snare line of measures 1–4 is now eight measures with the retrograde. We will repeat these eight measures to complete the sixteen measures needed for the piece.

The washboard line is eight measures. With its retrograde, the sixteen measures are completed.

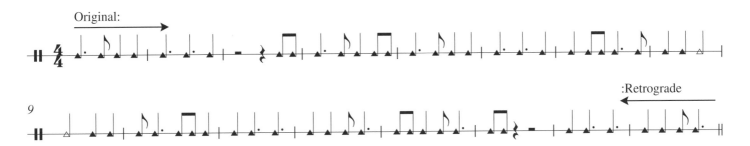

FIG. 9.32. Washboard Line. Measures 9–16 are in retrograde to measures 1–8.

Mensuration Canon for Percussion Trio

Putting the lines together:

- Snare drum: four measures, then retrograded and both repeated
- Washboard: eight measures and then its retrograde
- Bass drum: original line

FIG. 9.33. Mensuration Canon with Retrograde for Percussion Trio

ACTIVITY 9.3.

Write your own three-voice mensuration canon, twenty-four to thirty-two measures, using instruments with contrasting timbres and/or registers. Incorporate motivic manipulations in the original line and/or the subsequent imitative counterpoint (if applicable) of the faster moving lines.

SUMMARY

In this chapter, we defined and completed canons by augmentation and diminution, and applied the diminution procedure to transform "Row, Row, Row Your Boat" from a simple round into a mensuration canon. We then applied these skills to:

1. understanding Josquin's "Agnus Dei II" mensuration canon, and

2. constructing a modern mensuration canon with percussion instruments.

You then applied these techniques to writing your own original mensuration canon.

CHAPTER 10

Counterpoint and the Creative Process

Integrating counterpoint into musical compositions requires skill and inspiration. The contrapuntal techniques presented in chapters 1 to 9 can be applied to diverse musical styles and genres. The original examples included in this chapter were created by Berklee Online students as part of their studies while taking the counterpoint course. We will examine how these composers have applied multiple techniques across a broad range of styles. The examples demonstrate creativity combined with skillfulness to optimize one's compositional efficacy.

MOTIVIC MANIPULATION

In writing counterpoint, we often create a new melody (counterpoint) over a pre-existing melody (cantus firmus). Historically, these pre-existing melodies were often slowed down to provide a workable (melodic) baseline over which performers and composers, respectively, improvised or wrote new and quicker moving melodies.

As mentioned in chapter 3, the sixteenth century papal singer Costanzo Festa wrote 120 compositions over the slow-moving basse danse "La Spagna." You realized the last thirteen measures of this melody using motivic manipulation techniques to create imitative counterpoint.

The first example (figure 10.1) explores multiple transformations of one motive. Follow this one-measure motive and its sequences beginning with an inversion in measure 2, then with the addition of notes in measure 4 that is immediately sequenced down a step in measure 5. Measure 7 changes the first note of the motive while measure 8 uses rhythmic diminution to articulate the motive twice in straight eighth notes: first in inversion and then immediately followed in its original form (down a third from beat 1). Measure 9 is a retrograde inversion of measure 8 down a step. Measure 10 returns to its original form melodically and rhythmically (see measure 1), now down a fifth, and measures 11–13 slow down even further for the cadence using the retrograde inversion form in rhythmic augmentation beginning with F♮ and ending with F♯.

Audio 66

FIG. 10.1. Murat Kalaora's Setting and Analysis

(1) One-measure motive "a," stepwise motion

(2) Inversion of motive down a step

(3) Scalar descent: transition to motive "b"

(4) "b": modified sequence of "a" down a sixth with added notes

(5) Motive "b" sequenced down a step

(6) Changed first note for scalar ascent (a')

(7) Sequence with "a inverted" and "a" in rhythmic diminution more similar to "b"

(8) Retrograde inversion of measure 8 down a step

(9) "a" sequenced down a fifth

(10) "a" retrograde inverted sequence with rhythmic augmentation

The second "La Spagna" realization, by Andrey Borisov, uses harmonies of seventh and ninth chords with jazz inflected chromaticisms. Rhythmically, the counterpoint line is in syncopation with the cantus firmus articulations on the downbeat (see figure 10.2). The first two measures (see ① in figure 10.2) create a call-and-response relationship when measure 1 beat 4 asks a question with the tied quarter note of an ascending third (C to E), while measure 2 closes the phrase with a descending fifth (B♭ to E♭) that also acts as an anacrusis to the next two measures. Each measure contains a distinct motive, and they are frequently elided on the downbeat with syncopation. The first sequence in measures 3–4 (see ②) retains the basic rhythm and melodic contour of measures 1–2. It begins up a third but closes with a descending third (see ③) replacing the question of measure 1 with a comment. The second half of this sequence (measure 4) continues up a step instead of up a third (see ④), and the end of measure 4 replaces the previous sequence's closure with a question (ascending fourth, see ⑤) that now propels the music forward. The third reiteration of this two-measure phrase starts higher at measure 5 (E♭, see ⑥) but descends to G in beats 3–4 referring back to the G at the same place in the previous sequence (measure 3, beat 4). While the basic melodic contour of the motive in measures 2 and 4 is repeated in measure 6, the rhythms are now smoothed out to even eighth notes.

Ascending to F in measure 6, beat 3, marks the high point in this example and reminds the listener of the high points in the previous statements: D in measure 2 and then E♭ in measure 4. This creates a mid-ground relationship of ascending steps between these three two-measure melodic phrases. The fourth two-measure statement (measures 7–8, see ⑦) most clearly resembles its predecessor in measures 5–6, although the introduction of the quarter note in measure 8 slows down the music's momentum in preparation for the motivic changes in measures 9–13. The fifth and last sequence begins on measure 9 (see ⑧) but stops short in measure 10 (see ⑨) by repeating measure 9's rhythm while shrinking the intervals to step-wise motion. In measure 11 (see ⑩), the rhythmic and pitch material of measure ②, beats 1–2, reappears (down an octave), although the C is now C♯, clarifying its dominant tonal function. Beats 1–2 in measure 11 are immediately repeated in beats 3–4, and measure 12 (see ⑪) pares down the rhythmic and pitch material to a repeated syncopation of the dominant quarter note. In the final measure (see ⑫), the treble delays motion to the tonic, arriving on beat 3 after ascending through the upper tetrachord of the harmonic minor scale. This offsets expectations one last time but in the opposite direction—delaying rather than anticipating, pulling the listener forward for an extra two beats before the final resolution.

Audio 67

D minor tonality
with jazz
chromaticisms:

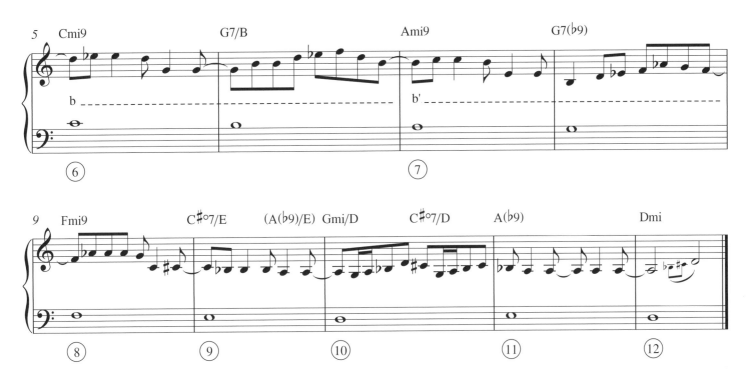

FIG. 10.2. Andrey Borisov's Setting

IMITATION OVER AN OSTINATO

In chapter 6, the chromatically descending bass ostinato in Purcell's "Dido's Lament," from his opera, *Dido and Aeneas*, provided a provocative ground on which you built at least two imitative melodic lines, with the option that these lines could be canonic.

Canon is a strict type of imitation in which the same music begins in a follower voice after the leader voice has started but before it ends. Within the original line, there are often multiple motivic manipulations. A free canon has modifications in the follower voice but retains enough similarities to the leader voice to be considered in canon.

Tim Nijenhuis' setting (figure 10.3) demonstrates motivic manipulations in the melodic lines with a two-voice free canon over the bass ostinato. The phrase structure and canonic lines overlap. This example demonstrates the advantages of using a free canon, that is, allowing plenty of room to depart from and return to the canonic technique while also using motivic modifications in a freer, imitative style.

PHRASES	MEASURES	CANONIC LINES
1	1–6	**Leader: m. 1–3** Follower: m. 3–5 • at the octave
2	6.3–11	Leader: m. 6.3–7.2, 9–13 • beginning on B♭ (dominant of E♭)
3	11–16	Follower: m. 8.3–9.2, 11–15 • beginning on E♭

FIG. 10.3. Tim Nijenhuis's Setting and Analysis

This next realization of Dido's "Lament" by Jeff Penny (figure 10.4) uses canonic imitation over the ground bass across four voices, each voice entering five measures after the previous voice. The cello first carries the ground in measures 1–11, and then the bass takes it over (measures 12–21) down an octave, for added gravitas. Violin II's canon, at the unison with violin I, enters at measure 6 and then the viola, down an octave, enters at measure 11.

After running the ground twice, the cello rests for a phrase and then enters, canon at unison with the viola, at measure 16. Harmonic clarity begins with the leader voice and ground bass (measures 1–5) and then is more fully revealed with two voices in canonic imitation (measures 6–11), then three (measures 12–16), and then four (measures 16–21). The resultant combination of rhythmic patterns that occur with each new entering voice maintains melodic independence of each voice through simultaneous diversity of rhythm even though there is diagonal (in time) rhythmic unison.

FIG. 10.4. Jeff Penny's Setting

JAZZ CANON BY INVERSION

In chapter 7, we explored canons at intervals other than the octave/unison and the inverted canon. The following example is an inverted canon at the sixth. It is in the jazz idiom, aptly demonstrating the diversity of the canonic applications across musical styles.

In Emily Jones's composition (figure 10.5), notice that the canonic line alternates between motion and rest. In this two-voice realization, the resting and moving passages alternate between the voices. This results in continuous forward motion in the foreground material while providing variety and novelty through registral and timbral contrasts. This is a canon at the sixth because the first note of the leader voice (G3) and the first note of the follower voice (E♭4) are a sixth apart. It is an inverted canon because the diatonically equivalent distance of every interval of the leader voice is maintained in the follower voice, but in the opposite direction. The third voice is a two-measure basso ostinato outlining the chord changes. The accompanying drum track on the audio is not notated in this example.

Inverted Jazz Canon at the Sixth

Emily Jones

FIG. 10.5. Inverted Canon at the Sixth, by Emily Jones. Audio (which includes an additional percussion track, not shown) produced by Emily Jones and used with permission.

DOUBLE CANON WITH INVERSION

The double canon, discussed in chapter 7, must have a minimum of four voices. Each pair of voices creates their own two-voice canon and the imitative relationship between the pairs of voices may be direct, as in the inverted canon at the third found in the Brahms "Canon No. 6" from the *Thirteen Canons for Women's Voices* (see figure 7.30), or it may be indirect as in freely imitative motivic relationships.

Contrapuntally, Ivan Jadresic's setting in figure 10.6 runs two canons, both starting on B. The first pair, violins I and II (anacrusis to measures 1 and 5, respectively), is four measures apart and at the unison. The second pair, cello and viola (anacrusis to measures 5 and 7, respectively), is also four measures apart but at the octave. Notice that the second canon is a melodic inversion of the first canon and closely models the Brahms example. Harmonically, these four corresponding contrapuntal voices fluctuate between modality and tonality until the very end. The opening leader line, in solo measures 1–2, sounds like E minor pentatonic. It continues in a G major tonality through most of the piece. The ambiguity between E minor and G major has been maintained, in part due to the avoidance of D♯ and the frequent use of D♮. When the D♯ appears for the first time at the penultimate measure (measure 15), it is a strong surprise—a novelty, revealing to the listener the tonal, rather than modal, orientation of the whole piece with the final closure in E minor.

FIG. 10.6. Double Inverted Canon by Ivan Jadresic

A CRAB CANON WITH A CONTEMPORARY ARRANGEMENT

The two voices in a crab canon switch places halfway through the canon (double counterpoint) and continue to the end by using their previous notes but in reverse order (retrograde), see chapter 8. Andrew Joslyn's setting in figure 10.7 demonstrates the crab canon technique with an audio rendition in a very contemporary musical style.

Audio 72

FIG. 10.7. Crab Canon by Andrew Joslyn. Audio produced by Andrew Joslyn and used with permission.

Canons of Rhythm

Canons of rhythmic diminution or augmentation are comprised of multiple voices, all singing the same melody, that move forward at different but proportionally related rates of motion (see chapter 9). These canons, including the mensuration canon, are one way in which pitches and rhythms are manipulated through repeating patterns or cycles. The use of repeating pitch and rhythmic patterns are not unique to the Western European classical tradition. The *taals* (rhythmic pattern) of Indian ragas (includes pitch pattern) existed over a thousand years before the European isorhythmic patterns of talea (rhythmic pattern) and color (pitch pattern) that led to the mensuration canon.

Eric Onasick's original composition in figure 10.8 applies the canonic and mensuration techniques of augmentation and diminution to a gamelan-inspired melody and includes an additional, non-canonic, percussion part. The first voice begins with two four-measure phrases, mostly in eighth-note rhythms and separated by contrasting registers. This eight-measure antecedent and consequent phrase pair is stated three times. The second voice enters at measure 9 in duple augmentation, playing the original four-measure phrase (now lasting eight measures in augmentation) twice. The third voice enters at measure 17 up a third and twice as fast, playing the original eight-measure pattern, now in four-measures, twice. One might imagine a turning wheel catching an inner wheel moving twice as slowly on its first turn around and catching the third, outer wheel, moving twice as fast, on its next turn around.

Audio 73

FIG. 10.8. Canon Using Mensuration Techniques by Eric Onasick. Audio produced by Eric Onasick and used with permission.

What are some other considerations for rhythmically proportionally related musical materials? For example, all voices in a mensuration canon begin with the same melody. But what if one applies proportional rhythmic patterns to different melodies? Could the rhythmic pattern itself continue to be heard as a unique musical identity? What if the articulations in the rhythmic pattern and the number of notes in the melody do not match so that the repetition of one pattern does not correspond with the other? Or, what if the rhythmic patterns are not proportionally related: can the same series of pitches continue to be heard as a melody when articulated with different, not proportionally related, rhythmic patterns? These, and other permutations have been continually explored by composers from the fourteenth century (see isorhythmic motets, composers Philippe de Vitry, Guillaume de Machaut) and into the twenty-first century (many styles including serialism and minimalism, and many composers including Pierre Boulez, Pauline Oliveros, and Philip Glass).

In these last examples (figures 10.9 through 10.12), students were free to use any of the contrapuntal techniques learned in the course. The following four compositions apply imitative contrapuntal techniques, in four contrasting styles. Each piece is musical as well as technically masterful and demonstrates how adaptable counterpoint can be for ones unique creative purposes.

The first free style piece (figure 10.9), titled "Leprechaun Night," by Anita C. Wood, evokes such Celtic images from its title, instrumentation including percussion, and the modally diatonic, Aeolian, melodies. The tom-tom ostinato line provides a strong metrical base while the auxiliary percussion line's ostinato (triangle and shaker) lifts up the rhythm with repeated syncopations.

In measures 1–8, all three melodic instruments move at various rates of speed: violin II moves the slowest, soprano recorder in the middle, and violin I the fastest. Their rhythms and pitches move in and out of unison, often with the effect of a brief echo or shadow as when the recorder joins the violin I's pitch an eighth note later. (See the solid and dotted lines annotated to the first phrase, figure 10.9). In the first half (measures 1–8), retrograde is the primary contrapuntal technique, with both voices restating their first phrase in retrograde (modifications are circled) in measures 5–8. The second half is freely imitative with the newly added rhythmic element of hemiola in measures 9–13. In each of those measures, one instrument is subdividing the measure into three beats, instead of two (see violin I in measures 9, 12, and 13; violin II in measures 10, 11, and 13).

In measure 10, the recorder inverts and modifies the motive in measure 9 and continues with a two-measure modified sequence (measures 11–12 to measures 13–14). The violins begin with double counterpoint in measures 9–10 to 11–12. In measure 13, they are simultaneously in inversion at the third and then violin II imitates violin I at the unison, one beat later, in measure 15. Cumulatively, this piece's intertwining rhythms and motives create a provocative interpretation of its title.

Audio 74

FIG. 10.9. "Leprechaun Night" by Anita C. Wood. Audio produced by Anita C. Wood and used with permission.

In a more chromatically progressive style, Julien Nodier's composition in figure 10.10 exquisitely demonstrates the application of multiple contrapuntal techniques combined with a good sense of melody within a chromatic and quartal idiom in a strong and cohesive form. This composition is influenced by Bartók's *Mikrokosmos*, and also carries some jazz-inspired melodic lines. The treble's opening statement in measures 1–2 continues as a canon at the octave in the bass voice, beginning at measure 3 and ending in measure 6. Both voices have now stated this chromatic and tuneful four-measure theme. Quartal harmonies support the second half of the theme in measures 5–6. The bass voice then repeats its previous four measures in measures 7–10, while the treble voice states most of the theme in retrograde. At measure 11, both voices present the second half of the theme at the octave with octave doubling and then repeat this in a sequence up a sixth (measures 13–14). The next three measures (measures 15–17) restate measure 1 in sequences: first down a seventh (measure 15), then up a fifth (measure 16, that is, up a fourth from the previous measure), and lastly at the octave (measure 17) with quartal harmonic support in the last two sequences. Those quartal harmonies articulate the final cadence through repetition and close with bass motion of a step while the treble voice leaps up a fifth.

FIG. 10.10. Bartók-Influenced Style by Julien Nodier

The next piece, by Juan Carlo Magsalin (figure 10.11), is a modern jazz realization of several contrapuntal techniques that flows smoothly through multiple counterpoints, harmonies, and rhythms with an end result that sounds effortless, as in its title: "Airborne."

The piece begins with a bass ostinato outlining the G Mixolydian mode. The main theme in the piano is imitated as an inverted canon at the third a measure later in the guitar. The canon continues through measure 9. Each measure (see score annotations) restates the measure 1 theme (or its inversion) at varying pitch levels to support the harmonic implications of the bass ostinato which itself is being sequenced down a step at measure 5, up a third at measure 7, and down a fifth at measure 9. The bass motion down a fifth in measure 10, from G to C, solidifies the first cadence as an authentic type even though the dominant itself is voiced quartally (G7sus).

In the B section, there are multiple contrapuntal techniques in both the piano and the guitar and bass voices. The left- and right-handed music of the piano in measures 11–12 are switched in measures 13–14 and, in so doing, create double counterpoint. However, this double counterpoint is not at the same pitch level: the right hand, in measures 13–14 is sequenced up a step (and an octave), and the left hand is sequenced down a seventh. Within each of these two measures, the left and right hands are also simultaneously performing the original and retrograde versions of this new motive, or theme, of the B section.

At measure 11 (section B), the bass begins with an arpeggiation that is repeated up an octave by the guitar a beat later in rhythmic augmentation. This two-measure pairing of arpeggiations is sequenced two more times beginning with the bass at measures 13, down a step; and 15, down another third. The rhythmic unison at measure 17 prepares for the half cadence (also quartal) at measure 18 and has moved back from E♭ Lydian to C Ionian. Section A is then repeated with rhythmic augmentation for the final cadence. Listen carefully to this example, and try to hear as many of these permutations as you can.

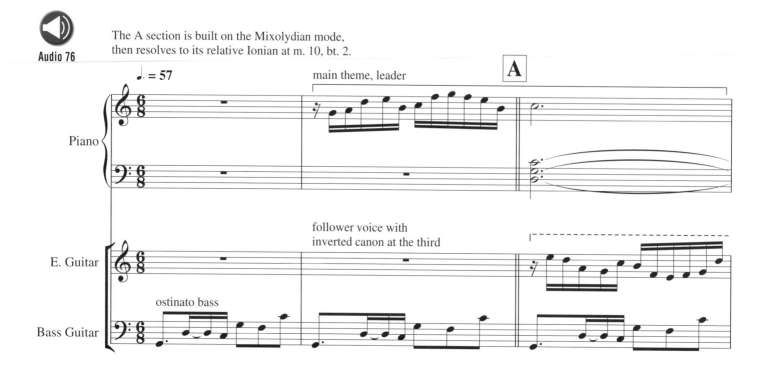

The A section is built on the Mixolydian mode, then resolves to its relative Ionian at m. 10, bt. 2.

main theme repeated (last note
adjusted down a step with ostinato)

main theme, sequenced down a step

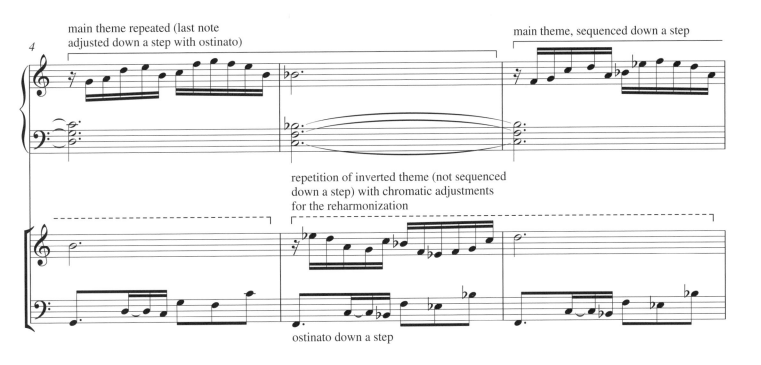

repetition of inverted theme (not sequenced
down a step) with chromatic adjustments
for the reharmonization

ostinato down a step

inverted theme, starts up a step from
guitar (m. 7), then modified for
approaching cadence

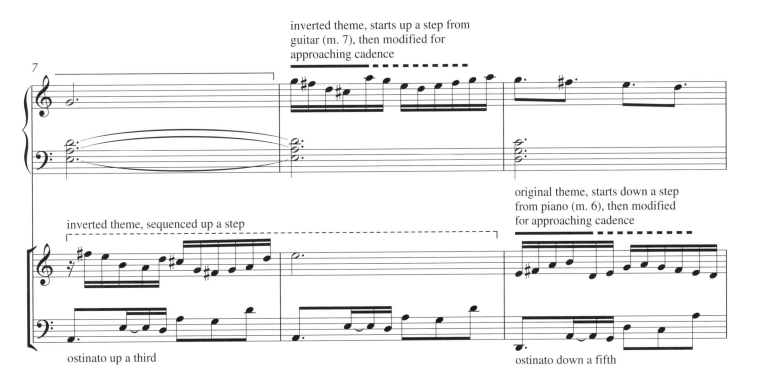

original theme, starts down a step
from piano (m. 6), then modified
for approaching cadence

inverted theme, sequenced up a step

ostinato up a third

ostinato down a fifth

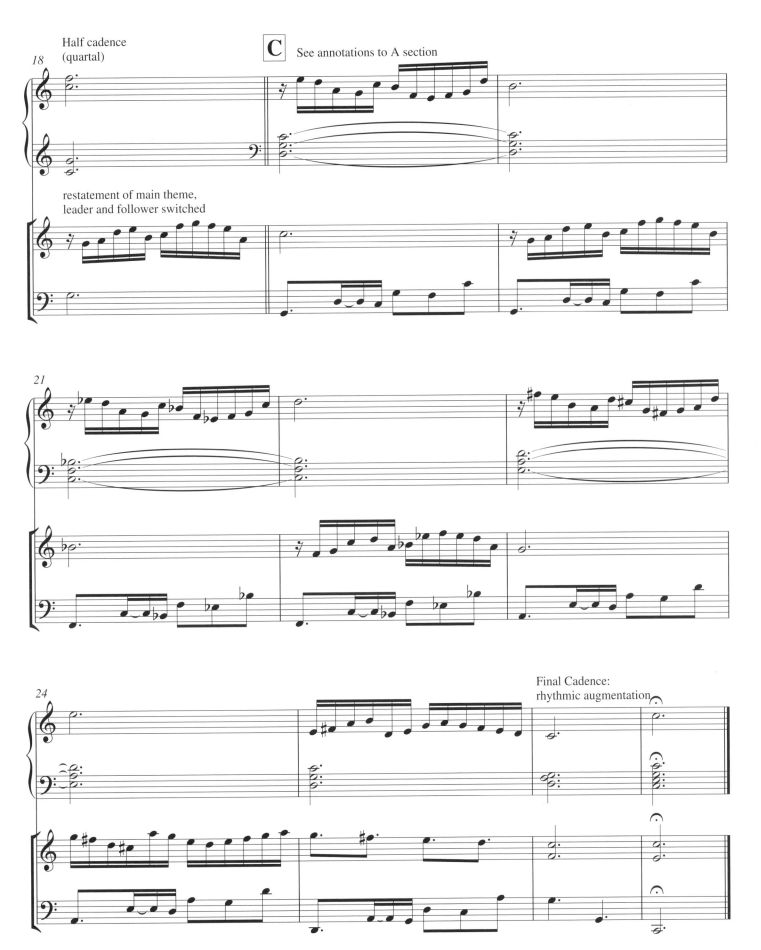

FIG. 10.11. Contrapuntal Piece in a Modern Jazz Style, "Airborne," by JC Magsalin. Audio produced by JC Magsalin and used with permission.

The final example, by Pat Cupo, demonstrates how a modern composer uses MIDI processes, resulting in a pictorial representation on the screen of the Digital Audio Workstation rather than the notation of a traditional score. In figure 10.12 the four pan drums in the background are in a mensuration canon creating a dense rhythmic texture. The bass part, a modified ostinato, repeats throughout with some pitch modifications. The prepared piano part is a canon in inversion at the m2 and flipped in retrograde at the midpoint as in a crab canon. The drums and piano both include a significant amount of reverberation/delay. On the piano part, this delay creates a four-handed two-piano effect that can be seen as part of the progressive end of the canonic imitation spectrum. All of the layers are connected by sharing one or more musical elements for a cumulative effect of linear imitation in multiple voices (counterpoint).

Audio 77

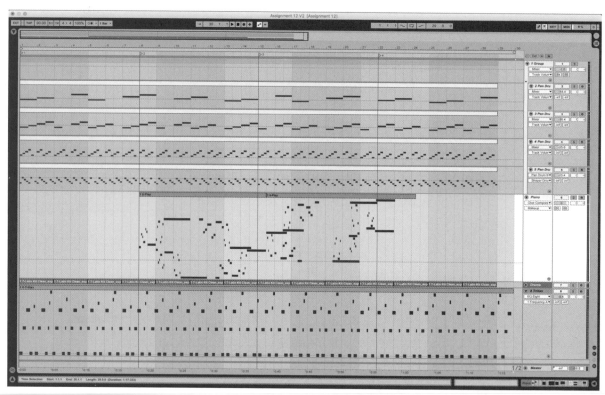

FIG. 10.12. Contrapuntal Piece in a Contemporary Production Style by Pat Cupo

AFTERWORD

As a classical composer moving through the traditional programs of music composition and theory, I learned the skills of the craft from a long line of styles that define the Western European tradition, stretching back almost a millennium. As a music teacher, I noticed that many of my theory students did not come to counterpoint with a familiarity of the historical styles. This disconnection was troubling and, I was confident, could be overcome.

A few years ago, Berklee encouraged me to develop a new way of teaching counterpoint that bridged the stylistic divide between contemporary musicians and the valuable skills of counterpoint inside those classical styles. The first result was my online course *Counterpoint*, which has proven very popular. We then developed this book both to support that course (available to any interested student, at Berklee or beyond) and others like it, and to serve as a resource for independent study.

Now that you have completed this book, use these techniques to work out your musical ideas creatively. Techniques are the servants of inspiration, and a well-equipped composer transforms that creative spark into an effective piece of music by using tools of the craft.

Wherever your career in music takes you—as a performer, composer, arranger, improviser, producer, songwriter, beat-maker, jingle writer, recording engineer—you now know how to make these compositional techniques your own. Revise and modify them to fit your needs, and "congratulations!" on expanding your musical horizons to include counterpoint.

ABOUT THE AUTHOR

Beth Denisch's music has been performed at Moscow's Concert Studio of Radio "Kultura," in Russia, at Jordan Hall in Boston, and Weill Recital Hall at Carnegie Hall in New York, across the U.S., and in Canada, China, Ecuador, Finland, Greece, Japan, and Scotland. Her music has received radio play and tracks are available online; CDs from Albany, Juxtab, Odyssey, and Interval record labels. Scores are published/distributed by Juxtab Music, ClearNote Publications, and TrevCo Music.

Denisch frequently draws inspiration from artists as well as authors such as Henry James in *Sorrow and Tenderness*, commissioned by the Handel and Haydn Society, and Jeanette Winterson, for *Jordan and the Dog Woman*, commissioned by the Equinox Chamber Players. Recently, she composed a multi-movement work for chorus and chamber ensemble on poems by Kathleen Jamie commissioned by the Concord Women's Chorus. Many ensembles and organizations have awarded Denisch including the Chamber Orchestra Kremlin in Moscow for *Fire Mountain Intermezzo*; Pennsylvania Academy of Fine Arts with the Philadelphia Classical Symphony for *The Singing Tree*, inspired by the Maxfield Parrish painting; and the Composers Guild for *Motherwell Lorca's Bagpipe Lament* (piano solo version). Other institutions that have commissioned and/or supported Denisch's music include the PatsyLu Fund of Open Meadows Foundation, American Music Center, Our Bodies Ourselves, and the American Society of Composers, Authors, and Publishers.

Denisch is professor of composition at Berklee College of Music where she teaches music composition and theory. She lives with her partner and two cats in Swampscott, MA.

- "…fierce rhythmic patterns," Bernard Holland, *New York Times*

- "…brimmed with personality and drive …" Anthony Tommasini, *The Boston Globe*

- "…wonderfully evocative … simply splendid," David Cleary, *New Music Connoisseur*

INDEX

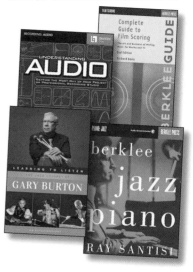